LOVE,
SURVIVAL,
AND
THE AMERICAN DREAM

GUSTA AND SOLOMON BERGER

jMo5000

Published by jMo5000
475 Washington Blvd.
Marina del Rey, CA 90292
USA

LOVE, SURVIVAL, AND THE AMERICAN DREAM
First edition, April 2013

Cover art by Julio Cano
Cover images used under Dreamstime.com license:
Real Stars at Night © by Peresanz
Stained Glass © 2010 by Palabra
Smith Museum of Stained Glass Windows © 2012 by Lisa Mckown

Typographic Design by Sarah Prochaska

Special thanks to Jeff H. Jarkow, Esq.
This book would not have been possible without your help.

For information about special discounts on bulk purchases,
book signings, or bringing an author to your event,
please contact jMo5000 at:
1-310-439-3737 or info@jMo5000.com

ISBN 978-0-9892469-0-3 (Paperback)
ISBN 978-0-9892469-2-7 (ePub)
ISBN 978-0-9892469-1-0 (Kindle)

CONTENTS

❧

PART I: LOVE

PART II: SURVIVAL

PART III: THE AMERICAN DREAM

PICTURES

❧

PART I:

ↄ

LOVE

 e/o

LOVE AT FIRST SIGHT

K rakow, April, 1945. A military bag with a change of clothes strapped over my right shoulder and a rifle strapped across my left. At my side, a bottle of vodka. As I had every day for the past year, I wore a personally tailored Soviet uniform. Instead of the normal green cap, I had a special black cap with a big red star. The first thing I did in Krakow was go to the Jewish Committee to register as a survivor of the war. This way, any of my family or friends who had survived would know that I was alive.

I did not have the slightest idea if anyone I knew had survived. I knew that my father had been killed. Two of my brothers had been taken to an SS training camp. My third brother had been with me until the liquidation of Krosno, Poland. This I knew. I did not know what had happened to my brothers after that. I suspected that my mother, sister, and two young nieces had not survived. The Germans took them away on August 10, 1942 to Belzec, a death camp.

In Krakow, the Jewish Committee was just a two-room apartment. A man sitting at the front desk looked at my Soviet uniform and hesitantly asked in Polish, "Who are you?"

"I want to see a representative," I responded. He took me to the other room to see the woman in charge. Junka sat behind a desk. She appeared twenty-five years old, the same age as me. I sat down in front of her desk. Before Junka said anything, I introduced myself. In my Soviet officer's uniform, I was out of place at the Jewish Committee. I said, "I am no Russian. My name is Solomon Berger. I am from Krosno. I survived with the Polish partisans as a Catholic for over a year and then was inducted into the Red Army." Junka listened and wrote down everything that I said. "I'm on leave right now…"

A beautiful blonde girl walked into the office. She walked over to Junka. They shook hands. They knew each other. The blonde girl was wearing a navy blue dress with white polka dots. She carried herself very innocently. She looked at me with her blue eyes like she was afraid to open her mouth.

"Don't worry about him. He is not a Russian," Junka said, "He is a Jewish man from Krosno. His name is Solomon Berger. He survived as a Catholic Pole. He is now serving in the Red Army under a pseudonym. You don't have to worry. You don't have to be afraid. You can talk freely."

I looked at this beautiful blue-eyed girl and said to myself, "I wish I could marry her. She is so beautiful." I fell in love the minute I saw her. The girl remained silent. I asked her, "Will you have lunch with me?"

"I don't go out with Russians," she responded.

"Junka told you already, I am not a Russian. I am Jewish."

"I am not having lunch with anybody." The girl walked closer to Junka. They had a brief conversation that I could not hear. The blue-eyed girl said goodbye and left.

I remained in the office. I asked Junka, "Who is that girl?"

"She is from my hometown of Tarnopol," Junka said. "Her sister was my friend. She is Jewish. Her original name is Gusta Friedman. She survived pretending to be a Catholic girl by the name of Stanislava Urbanska. Everyday, she comes to the Committee to see if her older sister, my friend Mina, survived in Germany. Just like you, she also would like to leave Poland, but she's afraid. She doesn't know anybody anywhere or have any money."

"Where does she live?" I asked.

"She lives in Krakow," Junka responded, "with a Polish woman and her husband who is an officer in the Polish army."

"Tell me her address," I demanded.

"I can't give you the address," Junka said. "I swore to her that I would not tell anybody where she lives…except her sister Mina."

"Where does she live?" I continued to demand.

"I cannot tell you! When Gusta told me her address, she made me swear not to tell anyone but her family!"

I did not give up. I continued to ask for Gusta's address. After Junka refused several more times, I insisted. My persistence paid off because Junka finally gave in. I said goodbye.

I waited at a safe house until nighttime because the curfew was still in effect. The war was still on. The people in Krakow could not walk in the streets after dark. As a Soviet officer, the curfew did not apply to me. I waited until after curfew so Gusta would be at home. That night, I walked to the address that Junka had given me. It was not far from the Jewish Committee. I wanted to tell Gusta, "I am going to desert the Red Army and leave Poland. I will take you with me if you want to go."

I knocked on the door.

A Polish woman answered. "Is Ms. Urbanska here?" I asked.

"We do not have a Ms. Urbanska here," she said and then tried to close the door on me. I stuck my foot firmly in front of the door. I saw Gusta in the middle of the living room. I pushed the door open and walked into the house pretending to be really angry.

"Why did you lie to me? Why did you tell me that she was not here?" I pretended to be a big shot. I pushed the Polish woman into her own bedroom, walked back to the living room, and approached Gusta.

"How did you know where to find me?" she said quietly.

"Junka gave me your address," I softly replied. As I looked at this beautiful girl I had already fallen in love with, I said, "I know who you are. I know that you want to leave Poland, but you don't have any money and are afraid. I also want to leave Poland. In the next day or two, a transport is going to leave from Krakow toward Romania, where boats are going to take a group of Jewish survivors to Palestine. If you want to leave, I'll take you with me. I will take care of you. You will not have to worry about a thing. If you want to go with me, meet me at the Jewish Committee tomorrow morning at ten o'clock." Without saying another word, I walked out of the house.

I did not wait for a response. This was wartime. I made decisions without considering the consequences. That night at the safe house, I wondered if Gusta would show up in the morning and thought about how this all began.

CHAPTER TWO

ℰᴗ

HISTORY OF SOLOMON

My first memory. I was three years old. Jewish kids in Poland had to go to nursery school at three. My father had a tailor shop with many people working for him. He told one of his workers, "Take Solomon to the nursery school!" I did not want to go and I did not let the worker take me. My father put me under his arm and carried me himself. I cried until he left me at the school.

My father's name was Jacob Berger. He was not a gentleman, but he was a very gentle man. He was also hardworking. He was a five-foot-three orthodox Jew with a small beard and yarmulke. He was born in 1865 in a small town called Korczyna close to Krosno in the Galicia region of southeastern Poland. In 1885, the Emperor Franz Joseph I of Austria lifted the prohibition of Jewish people establishing residency in the Galicia region. At twenty years old, my father was one of the first Jews to move to Krosno. Krosno had a population of fifteen thousand people. Two and a half thousand of them were Jewish. Right away, my father bought a house in the center of town. Three rooms and a kitchen. He designated two of the rooms for his tailor shop. The other Jews in Krosno also lived in the center of town. Most of the Poles lived on the outskirts or in the countryside. The Polish farmed two or three acres each. They raised cattle or pigs and had a lot of apple orchards. Every little piece of land was occupied. In the inner city, Jewish people were tailors, shoemakers, or carpenters. Krosno was a small town, but it acted like a big town. Even though Krosno did not have a large population, it had a glass factory, a refinery, and a galoshes factory. The factories also belonged to the Jews.

Soon after establishing himself as a tailor in Krosno, my father met a Jewish girl named Miriam Fabian who was also born in Galicia. They got married. Out of this marriage came five girls: first Helena, second Frances, third Bella, fourth Eleanor, and fifth Rose. Miriam died while giving birth to Rose.

According to the customs at that time, Miriam's youngest sister, Rosa Fabian, married my father to take care of the five girls. Rosa was seventeen years old and my father was already forty-seven. She was only a couple of years older than Helena. Out of this marriage came four sons. I was the third. My mother was a pretty woman. All throughout my childhood, I thought that she was blonde. When the Germans came in, she took her wig off, and I found out that she had strong black hair.

My oldest brother, Moishe, number six in the family, was born in 1913 in Krosno. In 1914, World War I broke out. The Russian Cossacks attacked Poland and came into Krosno. My father was inducted into the Austrian Army because Galicia belonged to Austria. My mother, already pregnant again and with five girls and two-year-old Moishe, evacuated to Hungary. In 1915, my brother Joshua was born in Budapest. My mother, five sisters, Moishe, and Joshua lived in Hungary until the end of the war. In 1918, my father was discharged from the army. He brought his whole family from Budapest back home to Krosno. My father and mother did not wait very long for somebody else to be born.

On October 28, 1919, I was born in Krosno, Poland. I was the first one in my immediate family to be born in a new Poland after its independence in 1918. One last brother, Michael, was born in 1921. Michael was the last of my father's children to be born and grow up. Our family consisted of five girls and four boys.

In the 1920s, my sisters started to leave Poland. An eighteen-year-old Frances and fifteen-year-old Eleanor left Poland for the United States. They settled in Chicago. Frances' boyfriend from Krosno, a tailor for my father, followed her to Chicago. They got married in America and had two sons. They lived in Chicago until 1936 when they moved to Los Angeles. Helena and Rose emigrated from Poland to Germany. Bella was my only sister who remained in Krosno.

HISTORY OF GUSTA

*M*y *earliest memory is something my mother said when I was fighting with my older brother, Benjamin, and my younger sister, Dora. As we fought, as young siblings always do, my mother came up to us. "Wait," she said kindly in Polish. "There will come a time when you will all want to see each other. There will come a time when you will all live in different villages or cities or countries. When that time comes, you will wish to see each other, to talk to one another, to enjoy each others' company. Do not fight. Please, do not fight."*

We stopped fighting.

My mother looked like me. My father looked like my oldest sister, Mina. We all had blonde hair and blue eyes. My mother was very pretty. She was tiny but my father was tall. His name was Moses and her name was Mirium. They had four children: Mina, Benjamin, me, and Dora. Our last name was Friedman. I was born on January 23, 1923, in an eastern Polish town called Tarnopol. On my birth certificate, my name is Gusta. My Jewish name was Gittle. When I came to America, they named me Gertrude, but I should have kept Gusta.

Two or three hours by train from Tarnopol was a village called Stefke. When I was little, I lived in Stefke with my mom, dad, brother, and younger sister on our farm. Mina lived in Tarnopol with our grandfather because three children was enough for my mother. My dad's mother died when I was only seven. I only remember her a little. My dad's father, my grandfather, lived in Tarnopol. I cry every time I remember him.

I never ate a strudel like my mother used to make. As a young child, I was not into cooking. I will always regret never learning how to cook from my mom. No matter how hard I try, I have never been able to make her cazel. When my family had soup, I do not remember matzah balls like I make now, only cazel. "Cazel," rhymes with "basil" and is like a cake but not a desert. It is made from potatoes. My mom baked grated potatoes in a clay pot. We sliced the cazel like bread and ate it with our soup. Chicken soup was the best.

My father's job was to watch all the people who worked on our farm in Stefke. There were no cows or animals on the farm, just land with corn and lots of other crops. Even though it was a big farm, we did not make much money. We did not have money to do anything fancy, only to live. Stefke was a small place. Only two thousand people lived in the town. There was a lot of open land. No mountains, hills, or forests. It did not snow in the winter.

I was a happy child. I traveled from my house to my Polish school in the town. I learned a little German and Russian. I understood German, but I never spoke it. I only spoke Polish. I knew how to read Hebrew because a teacher came to our house. At school, there were not many Jewish kids. My friends were both Jewish and Polish. Nobody ever gave me any trouble for being a Jew. We did not go to a temple. My grandfather was Orthodox, and I do not even think he went to a temple. I did not have a bat mitzvah. No girls had bat mitzvahs. Bar mitzvahs were only for boys. In Stefke, when a Jewish boy was thirteen, he went to the temple and that was it.

I do not remember if my brother, Ben, had a bar mitzvah. I do remember that he was handsome. He was tall and beautiful. My sister Dora was also beautiful. She had gorgeous blonde hair that was different from Mina's or mine. Only Dora's was thick.

We were never hungry on the farm and we all had many friends. When I was fourteen, I finished school and went to live in a big city called Lodz. I lived with my father's sister and her husband. Living with my aunt and uncle was like a summer vacation. Many friends from school were also in Lodz, so I always had someone to play with.

❦

CHAPTER FOUR

SOLOMON GROWS UP

I attended nursery school until I was six. The school, Hader, was only for Jewish boys. An old rabbi, with a beard and black hat, ran Hader. He taught us about the Torah. If we misbehaved, he spanked us. We had to behave. When I was five years old, I could already recite the five books of Moses. We were taught in Yiddish, the same language we spoke at home.

Our house did not have any running water or electricity, and the toilet was an outhouse. During wintertime, everything was frozen, so we used a tub in the house. Nonetheless, we managed to live quite happily. The River Wislok ran through our town. Every summer we swam in the river. In November, the snow came down and did not melt until April. We put on skis and skied straight out of the house and into the mountains. Krosno was at the foot of the Carpathian Mountains.

My siblings and I walked to the well every day and brought two buckets of water back to our house. We used this water for everything. To take a bath, we had to go to a public bathhouse once a week. We kept decently clean. We thought that this was how it had to be. At home, I always shared a room. We had double beds and slept five, six, or eight in a room. At nighttime, we burned natural gas for light. The oil refinery piped the natural gas directly into our house.

My father was a very devoted man. He worked six and a half days a week running his tailor shop. He sewed suits, coats, and everything that men wore. In those years, there were no ready-made clothes. All clothes had to be made to order by hand and foot-pumped sewing machine. Every Passover, we got new clothes from my father. He took off Friday nights and Saturday. Every Friday night and Saturday at noon, he brought two or three hungry people home from the synagogue to eat with us.

My mother worked very hard all the time to keep our household going. She managed to feed the household and tailor shop with the help of a live-in maid who lived in our kitchen. They made all our food by hand. My mother baked bread in the house while washing the laundry outside. She ground up meat and put bread in our soup so that there would be more to eat. We were never hungry. My mother had asthma, so every summer for a month she went to the Carpathian Mountains. Spending a month in the mountains helped her through her asthma and busy life.

At the age of six, I was enrolled in an ordinary elementary school next door to my house. When the school bell rang at eight o'clock in the morning, I jumped out of bed, grabbed up some pens, put on a pair of pants, and ran to school. After first period, I swung back to my house to have some breakfast.

Ten out of the fifty kids in my class at school were Jews. The rest were Catholics. Boys and girls got separated into two schools. Male teachers taught the boys and female teachers taught the girls. I had a different teacher for each class: history, Polish, chemistry, and Hebrew. All the Jewish kids studied with a Hebrew teacher outside of class for an hour each day while a Jesuit priest came into the school. Polish students studied under the priest who taught the Catholic religion. School was Monday through Saturday, but Jewish kids only went to school Monday through Friday. On Saturdays our teachers gave all the homework for the class, so the Jewish kids would fail. We knew what was going on. We got the homework out of the Polish kids on Sundays. At school, the Catholic priest had been teaching the Polish kids to hate the Jews. The priest taught them a lie that the Jews were responsible for killing Jesus Christ. I got into fights all the time. Even though I was short, I was one of the toughest. I gave in to nobody. In contrast, my younger brother Michael got beaten up. The school did not care because we did not fight in class. After the bigger fights, the parents got together and talked. My mother's only concern was that Michael and I got a decent education and completed seventh grade.

Michael and I were close. Our older brothers, Joshua and Moishe, were a little too old for us. They already had different friends. Michael and I grew up together. We were best friends, but I had many other friends. Solomon Moses was the closest. Everybody called him Solomon and me Shlomeck. Shlomeck became my nickname. Solomon's parents owned a big hardware store and a whole apartment building across the street from my house. When we left school at two o'clock, we went straight to Solomon's house to do our homework.

Everyday was homework. My favorite subject was history,

but I was the best at geography. I knew where almost every world capital was located. From third grade on, we studied at least two hours a week in German. The rest was in Polish. The minute we finished all our homework, we played soccer, skied, or swam. I was a hard runner. The only thing I never did was ice skate on the frozen river because the skates hurt my ankles. I played right defense on my soccer team, Gideo. We played against other Jewish teams, like Maccabee, and Polish teams too. The local Polish team, Vilegia, was stronger and beat us all the time. They had their own soccer field where we played. Tadeusz Duchowski was one of the best Polish players. His wife was good friends with my mother.

During the summer, we had two months off school. We played in the forests and had picnics. Without television and radio, there was nothing to do but play outside. We swam everyday in the River Wislok, which ran into the larger San River. When I was seven years old, I got my first bike with hand brakes and no gears. We rode bicycles to the nearby little towns to play soccer matches with other Jewish kids. Every ten miles was another little town with a different Jewish team. The dirt roads had no cars. People walked, bicycled, or rode a horse and buggy.

When we rode our bicycles to the next town, we took off our yarmulkes. Polish kids ran out to the roads and threw rocks and stones at us yelling, "Dirty Jews!" We were dressed just like they were and behaved just like them, but they hated us. We did not like them either. We tried to just walk away. Most young Jews my age wanted to leave Poland. There was no future for Jewish kids in Poland. We wanted to go to America.

In 1930, the economic crisis in the United States also hit Po-land. Nobody had any money to order clothes from my father's shop. I was hungry for the first time. My father, with all his workers, sat down in the tailor shop and had nothing to do. After a few weeks, a Polish customer suddenly came in and ordered three suits. We felt as if he had come from heaven.

Bella, my only sister who had remained in Krosno, married Raphael Yakobuvitch. Raphael was a sheet metal and glass man who could put anything together. He was also a musician who played violin at weddings. They had two daughters. The oldest called Sonya and the youngest called Manya. Bella, Raphael, Sonya, and Manya all shared one room in our house because they could not afford their own apartment.

When I was thirteen years old, my father took me to the synagogue in the morning. He brought a little vodka. I recited part of the five books of Moses. I read in Hebrew, but did not understand. That was my bar mitzvah. No parties. When I was thirteen, I also finished seventh grade. I wanted to go to high school, but Jewish kids were restricted. Additionally, high school had tuition, which my father could not afford. I still applied to high school. I was not accepted.

Instead, I enrolled at a private trade school in Krosno to become a bookkeeper. Over the next two years, I learned how to be an accountant with a dozen other students. After graduation, I could not get a job. Nobody needed any young bookkeepers. My father said, "You are sixteen years old. Nobody needs a young accountant. You need to find a trade. I have a tailor shop. I have work for you. If you learn to be a tailor, it will save you from two things in your life: you'll never get rich and you'll never starve." So, my father taught me tailoring. I also went to a tailoring trade school in Krosno to learn design and pattern making.

I finished tailoring school in 1935 and started to work for my father. In 1936, I walked up to my father and said, "I'm leaving." I was sixteen. I hitchhiked to Krakow.

CHAPTER FIVE

INDEPENDENCE

I went to Krakow because it was bigger than Krosno. There were one hundred thousand Jews out of a population of two hundred and fifty thousand in Krakow. I easily found a place to live with four other boys in the Jewish section for a few cents a month. I got myself a tailoring job making vests for fifty cents a day. I ate twenty-five cent dinners at a public kitchen. Somehow, I survived.

I supported myself in Krakow for a year. I only went out to the tailor shop or the Maccabee sports club to play ping-pong, soccer, or box. I learned how to defend myself. There was no television. I could not afford to go to the talking movies that were just catching on. Sometimes, I was hungry. My mother kept sending me letters that said, "It's time to come back home. You have made your point." I let my mother beg because going home was all I wanted.

In 1937, I arrived back home in Krosno. I resumed tailoring for my father with my three brothers in our crowded house. Joshua, Michael, and I wanted more space and privacy, so we built another room in our tall roof. We were happy to each have our own straw sack to sleep on in the attic.

After working all year for my father, I took the summer off. That summer, I went to a camp with a small group of other Jewish teenagers. We started training for a right-wing military organization called Beitar. Beitar's Polish leader was Menachem Begin. He later became the prime minister of Israel in 1977. Beitar's plan was to fight the British in Palestine and liberate an independent Jewish state. During the summer, a retired Polish army sergeant taught us to use rifles and throw hand grenades. We also practiced hand-to-hand combat.

I had always wanted to fight for a Jewish state. I wanted to get away from Poland because Jews were citizens without rights. Jews could not buy any land or have government jobs. We had to live in certain places. When Polish hooligans attacked us, the police did not do anything. Jews got to vote, but the government was anti-Semitic. The Polish prime minister said, "We do not have room for three and a half million Jews. One million is enough. The rest can leave." Practically every Jewish kid belonged to a Zionist movement.

In my house, we all had different ideas. My father was never involved in politics. He just listened. He spoke only Yiddish and signed his name with an "X." But his four sons all belonged to different political organizations. My oldest brother Moishe, a Hasidic Orthodox, belonged to a Jewish religious organization called Agudat Yisrael. They just wanted to study Torah. They were against a Jewish state in Palestine until the return of the Messiah. Joshua belonged to a Zionist left-wing organization called Poale Zion that wanted to immigrate to Palestine to form a Jewish kibbutz or community. They wanted a Jewish state, but did not want to fight. Michael belonged to Hashomer Hatzair, an ultra left-wing organization that bordered on communism. During Shabbat dinner on Friday nights, we often argued. My brothers called me the fascist, like Mussolini, but I did not care. I persisted that it was best to go to Palestine to fight for an independent Jewish state. I always won the arguments at the dinner table. Even though we argued, all our organizations had the same plan: leave Poland.

After the summer was over, I returned to work for my father, but I continued to train with Beitar. On weekends, I went on picnics in the forest with boys and girls from Zionist organizations. We sang and ate bread, butter, milk, and hamburgers. I dated one girl, but it was nothing special. I was a teenager.

In 1938, my sisters in America sent us a letter asking us to join them. "I am not leaving Poland," my father told the family. "I am not leaving my town. This is where I was born. America is not a kosher country." He continued, "Children, if you want to leave, go ahead and leave." Michael, Joshua, and I wanted to leave, so my sister Frances sent us an affidavit of support. We registered for immigration at the American consulate in Warsaw, but America had an immigration quota for the eastern part of Poland. We were scheduled to be considered sometime in 1942. In the meantime, I wanted to go to Palestine.

In 1938, I had to register for the Polish draft. As much as the Poles hated us, they still made us register for the army at the age of eighteen. I could then not get a passport. I was stuck in Poland.

e/o

THE KRISTALLNACHT

November, 1938. My sister Rose's husband, Jack Landerer, came to Krosno after being deported from Germany. He told us that during the night of November 9, Gestapo, SS, and ordinary Germans ran wild burning Jewish synagogues. They burned Jewish schools and destroyed Jewish homes. They burned books that were published by German Jewish scientists. The SS, German Nazi paramilitary forces with police powers, attacked Jews in the streets. Jack called it "the Kristallnacht," the night of the broken glass.

Jack explained that the Gestapo and the SS had launched a series of coordinated attacks, a pogrom, against the Jews on the Kristallnacht. The Gestapo, the Nazi secret police, arrested thousands of Jewish people and incarcerated them in a concentration camp called Dachau. The Germans had started to arm themselves for a conquest of Europe.

"The day after the Kristallnacht," Jack said, "Rose went to visit her oldest sister, Helena, in a Berlin hospital because Helena was supposed to have surgery. At the hospital, Rose was told that Helena had died during the Kristallnacht. No one knew how she died."

Jack was Polish but ran a tailor shop in Berlin. After the Kristallnacht, he was rounded up with other Polish Jews working in Germany and deported back to Poland without his family. His wife, my sister Rose, was pregnant again and remained in Berlin with their daughter, Marilyn. Rose was a very resourceful woman. She went to the Gestapo in Berlin and got Jack a transit visa to return from Poland to Bremerhaven, a German port. She also obtained affidavits of support from our other sisters in America and was able to obtain United States visas for her family. Visas were also obtained for Arnold, Marion and Sigmund Gable, the two teenage children and widower of my sister Helena. Jack met the group in Bremerhaven, and they all boarded a German freight ship. Rose gave birth to a son while still in German waters. The German captain named the baby boy Sheldon. The freight ship sailed for six weeks straight through the Panama Canal to Los Angeles, California. They had departed Germany two months before the war started.

The Polish press told us nothing about what was happening in Germany. After hearing about the Kristallnacht from Jack, we were scared of what the Germans could do. The Polish government propaganda told us that Poland was strong and that the Germans were starving and weak. If Germany attacked, Poland would destroy them with its cavalry. We believed the propaganda. Nobody ever believed that Hitler had a plan to destroy the Jewish people.

I continued working as a tailor at home and training in the park with Beitar. The Poles did not bother us. We were not a large force. I ate at home with my family. Fresh bread with butter and milk in the morning. For dinner, which was lunchtime, a soup with meat and dried fruit. At night, a piece of bread with butter and tea. Coffee was very expensive. I read books by Alexandre Dumas. The Three Musketeers was my favorite. I read Tolstoy in Polish. I spoke Yiddish at home with my parents, brothers, sister, nieces, and my brother-in-law, Raphael.

Middle of August, 1939. The Polish government started to play war music on the radio. They announced that Nazi Germany was preparing for war. We did not have a radio in our house, so I listened at Solomon's or at a business. Krosno first got radios about seven years before, when a German man set up a radio shop in town. A week before September, the Polish army recalled my brother Joshua from the reserves. Joshua left to rejoin the Polish army.

The last days of August. The Polish government selected block captains for wartime. We had to cover our windows so that the Germans could not see any lights. We used strips of paper. If we were attacked, the glass would not spread.

We prepared for war.

PART II:

∾

SURVIVAL

CHAPTER SEVEN

௭

WORLD WAR II BEGINS

Five thirty in the morning. I woke up to the sound of explosions all over town. I covered my ears and waited in the attic with my brothers for fifteen minutes until it stopped. We did not know what was happening. It was Friday, the first of September, 1939.

We left the attic and went out into the streets. It was light out and the whole city was on fire. I walked five minutes to the square by city hall where there were radios. "Nazi Germany has attacked," an announcement said. "The Germans have crossed the Polish border. We are at war."

The German air force knew right where to attack in Krosno. They bombed the glass factory. They bombed the refinery. They bombed the galoshes factory. Word got around that the German who had set up the radio shop was a spy. The Germans did not have to ask us for directions. I learned that they were coming from Czechoslovakia across the Carpathian Mountains. Their ground forces would be in Krosno in two days. Poland had a cavalry army from World War I. The Germans were coming with motorized tanks.

Nobody had any idea that the Germans were going to come in and kill people without any reason. Nobody expected that. We all believed that Germans were educated people. My parents remembered that the Germans treated civilians very well when they took over the southeast territories during World War I. They thought that it was going to be the same this time.

The next day, the Polish army retreated eastward. They ordered all young people of military age to come with them. Michael and I, along with a small group of eight other young Jews retreated with the Polish army. People were running around and did not know what was going on. My group retreated ahead of the advancing German army. They constantly bombed us. German planes dove down and fired their machine guns. We jumped into ditches on the side of the road. Bullets flew all around me.

Every ten miles was another little town. We stopped at old people's houses for food and continued walking twenty miles east every day. All young people were trying to get as far away from the German army as possible. We heard a rumor that the Germans were using gas bombs. From then on, whenever we heard planes flying overhead, we urinated on pieces of cloth that we then put over our mouths to protect us from the gas bombs. It tasted terrible, but we had to survive. Everything was new and strange. Luckily, nobody in my group was injured.

After retreating for seven days, the German tanks finally caught up to us. We were one hundred miles east of Krosno, near the city of Lwow. Two or three tanks traveled together. They fired a handful of rounds wherever they went. We jumped into ditches. I could feel the vibration of the tanks as I waited for them to pass. There was no use running anymore. We learned that the

Soviets had crossed the border into eastern Poland. The Polish army was trapped between the Germans and the Soviets. Poland was surely defeated. All we could do was go back home. The German army stood between us and Krosno. We knew that questions were going to be asked. Our group selected a spokesman. I was selected because I could speak the best German.

We walked west for several days. Twenty miles from Krosno, two German military police on a motorcycle with a sidecar approached. It was late afternoon. The two Germans got out of their sidecar motorcycle and pointed machine guns at us. I had seen SS troops killing Jews indiscriminately. I stepped in front of my group. The officers walked up to me. "Who are you?" they asked me in German.

I lied to them in German with the first thing that came to my mind, "We are descendants of German nationals," I said without hesitation. "Our parents have lived in Silesia for many years. We were ordered to retreat with the Polish army. We want to go back home."

Chapter Eight

ᕽᕽ

BLACK MARKETEERING

"You can't walk on the street now. It's curfew time," the German officers said. "We will escort you now to a building where you will stay overnight." The officers seemed to believe my story. The Germans escorted us to an empty school building. "We will be back in the morning to take you home," they said. After the officers left, our group decided that we would not wait for them to come back. The Germans would find out who we really were. We decided to leave at daybreak.

I fell asleep right away on the wooden floor. The minute it became light, we escaped from the school building. We walked all day and night toward Krosno. When we arrived the following day, my family was overjoyed to see Michael and me.

Krosno was destroyed. Nazi Germany had attacked from the west, the Soviets had attacked from the east, and Poland had disintegrated in only three weeks. German soldiers constantly rode through town on trucks like winners. They were all dressed beautifully in comparison to the Polish soldiers. The Germans were advancing to the east.

In Krosno, nobody worked. Nobody knew what was going to happen. We all hoped that everything would be okay. Within two weeks, Nazi Gestapo arrived in Krosno. They immediately arrested the city mayor and all the city councilmen. Nobody ever saw them again. The Gestapo took over Krosno's government. They established a Jewish Committee to relay orders to the Jews. The Gestapo conducted a mandatory census to create a list of all the Jews in Krosno: where we lived, our ages, our professions.

Following the Gestapo came the SS, which the Germans called "occupation forces." The SS wore ordinary grey German army uniforms. However, they wore special black caps with a skull and crossbones insignia on the front. From the moment the SS arrived in Krosno, they indiscriminately beat and killed Jewish people. I watched through my window as the SS dragged people out of their homes and shot them in the street.

After a week of countless murders, the Jewish Committee announced that the Gestapo would allow Jews to leave German-occupied territory to go to the Soviet-occupied territory east of the San River. We had to provide our own transportation. Michael and I decided to leave for the Soviet side. We figured the Soviet side could be beautiful and completely different. We wanted our parents to come with us. My father said, "We are not leaving. We are going to stay here. It's not so bad. You children go. You children go and hopefully everything will be alright." Only Michael and I wanted to go to the Soviet side. "You children go," my father told us, "nobody is going to touch us, we are old people. You children go when you're young. Start a new life. Go. And may God be with you."

The next day, Michael and I joined my friend Solomon Moses, his family, and half a dozen other young Jews. Solomon's family paid a farmer to take us in his wagon twenty-five miles southeast to Sanok, on the San River. East of the river, we would be out of German territory. I only had a change of clothes and very little money. I felt terrible because my family was breaking up. We all hoped that Hitler was going to lose. England and France had declared war against Nazi Germany three days after the invasion of Poland. We hoped that England and France would defeat the Germans. We hoped to come back to Krosno. After three and a half hours in the back of the open buggy, we reached Sanok.

The San River was large, but not deep. When we walked across, the water came up to our knees. Soviet border police waited for us on the other side. The Soviet police were not as nicely dressed as the Germans. They were mostly Ukrainians dressed in brown uniforms who spoke to us in Ukrainian which was close to Polish. A policeman said, "You can't stay here. We don't want any refugees in the border area. You have to go deeper into Soviet territory. You will be transported east to Sambir where you will be permitted to live."

We walked with wet pants and soaking shoes to the nearby village. The villagers gave us food and water. We spent the night sleeping on the ground. The next day, we boarded trucks with other refugees and traveled a couple hours east to Sambir. We stayed in a community building with lots of rooms and fifty other refugees. We slept on the floor or on cots, but there was plenty of room. We could not take regular baths. Everybody got lice. It was really itchy. We did not have disinfectant to get rid of the lice, so all that we could do was try to clean ourselves in the nearby river. The river was cold and we did not have any soap.

We came to the Soviet side because we thought they were living a beautiful life in a socialist country. After only a few days in Sambir, we realized that the people actually had nothing. Even the Soviet soldiers seemed to have nothing except for lots of rubles. Michael and I learned from other refugees that the soldiers would buy practically anything. Michael and I went to street vendors to buy whatever we could afford. We sold it for double the price to the Soviet soldiers. If we bought three yards of cloth for fifty rubles, we could sell it for one hundred rubles to the Soviets. We purchased clothes and jewelry, but we always hoped to buy watches. A watch was worth more than anything else for the Soviets. They would even buy a broken watch because they were so crazy about watches.

At least we were not afraid for our lives, like in German-occupied territory. The Soviets did not interfere with us, unless we involved ourselves in politics. A special division of Soviet forces called the NKVD, which later became the KGB, patrolled the population for anti-communist activities. The NKVD monitored every building to keep track of anyone who entered and left. If several people entered a building where they did not live, the NKVD knew that there could be a meeting. The Soviets put up political posters all over town. One showed a rich man standing behind a peasant with a whip and read, "This is how it was." A second picture showed the same peasant raising his head and throwing away the rich man's whip, "This is how it will be," it read. I was not involved in politics but still tried to find out what was happening.

One day, Michael was selling some items to a Soviet soldier.

"Why aren't you fighting the Germans?" I asked the soldier.

"There was a secret agreement between Molotov, our foreign minister, and von Ribbentrop, the German Nazi foreign minister," the soldier explained. "Molotov and von Ribbentrop agreed in 1939 that they were both going to occupy Poland. Nazi Germany attacked Poland from the west and the Soviets attacked from the east. After defeating Poland, Nazi Germany and the Soviet Union divided the country according to their agreement."

A month later, Michael met a girl whose parents owned a grocery store. Michael convinced the girl to let us stay at their house. She made the arrangements with her parents. The house had four rooms next to their grocery store. It was a small family with plenty of food, so it was not a problem for Michael and me to live with them. We ate a lot of bread and potatoes. There was very little meat, but nobody was hungry.

Michael and I wanted to find more things to sell to the Soviets in a larger town. We went to the Sambir railroad station. While waiting for our train, we heard somebody yell, "Shlomeck! Mikeal!" We turned around to find our brother Joshua in a Polish uniform! Michael and I had found our lost brother who had gone to war. "The Polish army has disintegrated," Joshua told us. "The Soviets are taking Polish soldiers to prison war camps." Joshua snuck off with us and threw away his Polish uniform. We three brothers went back to the house. The girl and her parents agreed to let Joshua stay.

In December of 1939, we heard that the Soviets were recruiting young people to work in the coal mines in Donbass, Ukraine. Michael and two of his friends decided to go. Joshua and I did not want to go. Even though the Soviets promised good wages, I was doing fine. Michael, who was very short, and his two friends, who were very tall, left to work in the coal mines. The next day, Michael returned to Sambir with a cough and a temperature. "What happened?" Joshua and I asked him.

"My friends and I had to stand in line all night to register," Michael responded, shivering. "It was twenty degrees below zero and none of us were prepared. When the door opened in the morning, the Soviet commissioner happened to be Jewish. The commissioner started to register all the young people. When our turn arrived, my friends were approved and registered. The commissioner looked at me and said, 'You don't belong here. You won't last two years underground working the coal mines looking like you do right now. Go back home.'" Michael had contracted pneumonia while standing in line all night in the frost. No medical care was available. Michael would die if he did not get the care of our parents or a nice home.

We found out that Polish smugglers snuck people back and forth across the border at the frozen San River. The smugglers were mostly Polish farmers who had safe houses to use during transport. Joshua and I hired a smuggler to take Michael across the border and back to our parents in Krosno. Two weeks later, the smuggler came back to Sambir with a piece of cloth from our father as proof. Joshua and I wanted to smuggle our parents and the rest of the family back to the Soviet side. It was safer than on the German side. The next week, Joshua and I, along with six other young Jews, hired a smuggler to take us back to German-occupied Poland. We decided to leave on New Year's Eve when there would be many parties. The Soviets would be drunk and the Germans would be celebrating.

After midnight, it was January 1, 1940. We met with the smuggler at a safe house. We quietly walked west through snow and ice to the frozen banks of the River San. We started to walk across.

✌️

Chapter Nine

FROM BAD TO WORSE

The German and Soviet border police would both shoot at anybody who crossed the river. We calmly reached the other side. Now in German-occupied territory, the smuggler dropped our group off at a safe house to sleep for a few hours. In the morning, a different smuggler hid us in the back of a horse and buggy.

New Year's Day, 1940. We arrived back home in Krosno. Everybody was very happy to see Joshua and me. The whole family was back together. Unfortunately, our happiness did not last long.

It was a big mistake to come back. Krosno was completely different and much worse than the Soviet side. In German-occupied Krosno, Jews did not have freedom. The Gestapo restricted our movements, shut down our schools, and burned our synagogues. Jews were not allowed to pray together. Jewish boys and non-Jewish girls could not meet. We were not allowed to know anything about what was happening in the world. Jews could not have radios or newspapers. The Gestapo restricted everything.

Jewish people had to wear a white armband with a blue Star of David. The Gestapo knew who every Jew was from the census. They did not have to guess who was a Jew. We even had to provide our own armbands. I sewed a blue Star of David on a piece of white cloth from my father's tailor shop. Every time I went outside, I tied it around my right shoulder. SS beat up or shot Jews in the street without armbands. SS and Gestapo immediately beat up any Jewish person they came across on the sidewalk who did not get off the sidewalk, take off his cap, and bend down in respect. Jews were murdered if they resisted, but if Catholic Poles resisted, they were only beaten up. Jews were shot in open daylight for no reason at all. SS and Gestapo buried their victims as a normal procedure. They did not need a justification to kill.

In the beginning, ordinary German soldiers were not the killers, it was the SS and Gestapo. There were half a dozen Gestapo in Krosno. One Gestapo named Baker was a real murderer. Baker was a Polish citizen, but a German national. He was six feet tall, slim but muscular. He could be described as a handsome forty-year-old man. When the Germans took over Krosno, Baker volunteered for the Gestapo and became a plain, ordinary murderer. He took Jewish people down to the closest field and told them to dig themselves a grave. He then took out his gun, fired, and killed the Jews into their own graves. It was a daily procedure.

All Jewish youths were ordered for compulsory labor under the supervision of the SS. The work orders came from the Jewish Committee, who established a special police for Jews. The Jewish police did not have weapons and wore a special armband in addition to the normal Jewish armband. We had to follow the orders of the Jewish police to go to slave labor.

At eight o'clock in the morning, we had to assemble in the town square. The Jewish police conducted a role call of all young Jewish men. If anybody was missing, they knew exactly who it was. The Jewish police would tell the SS who then went to the missing person's house. SS dragged that person out of his house and beat or shot him. Moishe, Joshua, Michael, and I were always on time for roll call. My father did not have to go because he worked as a tailor from home for the German military service. Raphael also did not have to go because he did glasswork, sheet metal work, or other handyman work for the German military service. The women and children stayed at home.

After role call, we found out how many workers the SS needed for the day. The SS usually requested about one hundred workers at a time. Under the direction of the SS, my brothers and I shoveled snow, loaded and unloaded military trains, and worked at the airport. The Germans constructed completely new highways to replace the dirt roads in Poland. We did the manual labor before professionals laid down the cement. We were not paid. If we did not bring food from home, then we did not eat. The SS called us "you pig-dogs" in German. We worked ten hours a day with the fear of being shot at any moment.

The SS permitted us to live at home with our parents, which helped us survive. We could wash up, eat, and rest before reporting back to work the next day at eight o'clock in the morning. Sunday was our only day off. On Sundays, we rested. Our backs hurt and we were sore all over. We were not used to doing dirty work with our hands.

Joshua and I quickly realized that we could not smuggle the family back to the Soviet side. Furthermore, by February,

German and Soviet armies completely occupied the borders. Neither side would let anyone cross. If anybody tried to cross the River San, both sides would shoot.

As my brothers and I continued to report to slave labor, I saw that my friends on the Jewish police did not have to work. By joining the Jewish police, I could save my family from a lot of discomfort. When I told my family that I wanted to join the Jewish police, they all jumped at me. "Nobody in our house is going to collaborate with the Germans!" they all said.

"But I want to save you from being dragged to work!" I replied.

"We will go to work," my father said. "We will do what anybody has to do. Nobody is going to be a policeman for the Germans from our house. If you insist on becoming a policeman, then get the hell out of the house!" My family was right. I did not join the Jewish police.

One day my brothers and I were working at the German military airport carrying wooden boards that were so heavy that three people were needed to carry one. A German air force sergeant, who was not an SS, guarded us. Unfortunately, my brother Moishe was lazy and instead of holding his part of the board, he bent down so that the weight would lie on somebody else's shoulder. The German sergeant noticed Moishe's behavior and started to beat him. "You are lazy. You're not allowed to do that," the sergeant said.

I walked over to the sergeant and said, "Why are you hitting him? Why don't you leave him alone?"

"It's none of your business," the sergeant replied.

"He is my brother."

"You're not in charge here. Go back to work before you get yours."

"You try."

The sergeant pushed me. He was big and more than six feet tall. I was only five-foot-four and one hundred pounds. I clenched my right hand in a fist and hit the sergeant in his chin. I knocked the sergeant to the ground with one punch. He got up and grabbed his gun from his holster. He pointed it straight at my face and got ready to shoot me. "Get back to work!" he yelled. "If you don't get back to work right now, I'm going to kill you."

I went back to work and the sergeant put his gun back in his holster. The rest of the day, I felt terrible. I decided that I could not stay in Krosno working for the Germans. I could not comply with their orders. I would escape. That night, I told my brothers, but they all said, "We are staying. We are afraid to escape. We are not going anywhere."

CHAPTER TEN

⟡

A NARROW ESCAPE

June, 1940. I started organizing young people to escape from
Poland. The dozen young Jews in my group met at different
hiding places every few nights in Krosno. We wanted to book
passages on ships in Romania and sail on the Black Sea toward
Palestine. As we made preparations to escape the Nazis, we learned
that we needed American dollars to pay for the ship transportation.
We also learned that we could get American dollars from a black
market foreign money dealer in Tarnow, a Polish town larger than
Krosno. As leader of the group, I would travel to Tarnow to buy
American dollars with the group's Polish money.

I took an early train, traveled forty miles northwest, and arrived
in Tarnow for the first time in the late morning. I started toward
the money dealer. Tarnow was strange and unfamiliar. As I walked,
I bumped into a young man wearing a white armband like mine.
I recognized him as a member of Beitar. We had trained together.

"What are you doing here today, Shlomek?" he asked me.

Since I had known him for quite a while, I decided to confide in him, "I came to Tarnow to purchase American dollars. I want to escape to Palestine with a small group of Jews."

"What time are you going back to Krosno?"

"Probably on the afternoon train," I told him. We said goodbye to each other and parted ways. I continued on to the money dealer and purchased enough American dollars to book ship passages for my entire group. It was not safe to carry the currency, so the money dealer and I arranged for his twelve-year-old daughter to take my American dollars to the railroad station and hand it off when the train arrived.

In the afternoon, I arrived back at the Tarnow railroad station. The young man from Beitar was also at the station. "What are you doing in here?" I asked.

"I came to see you off," he said and left.

Two Gestapo officers walked over and immediately arrested me. I suspected that the young man from Beitar was an informer for the Gestapo and had pointed me out. Fortunately, the twelve-year-old girl had not yet given me the American dollars.

"Where is your American money?" one of the Gestapo asked in Polish.

"I don't have any American money," I said. "I never had any American money." The two Gestapo punched me on both sides of my head and my ears. I went briefly deaf after their blows.

The next thing I knew, I was inside a military building. The same two Gestapo walked me down a hallway. A door was open, and I saw the money dealer's daughter in a room. I was taken to an empty room. The Gestapo closed the door and began to hit me again. In Polish, the officers asked, "Who else is involved in anti-German activities?"

"I did not do any money dealing," I said. "I had nothing to do with this. I do not have any American dollars."

"Who else is involved in your black marketeering?" they demanded. "Who else is involved in your black marketeering?"

I did not admit anything. They hit me with a rubber stick and kicked me when I was down. They continued to interrogate me with the same questions and beat me when I did not give them answers. My whole body, from one end to the other, was black and blue. After two hours, one of the Gestapo said to the other in German, "He doesn't want to tell us anything. We will come back after he gets some rest. If he won't tell us anything, he better know what's waiting for him." The Gestapo did not know that I understood German. Then I was alone in the interrogation room.

Lying in a corner all beaten up, I knew that the Gestapo were coming back to kill me. I pulled myself up from the ground and noticed that there was a small, lightly barred window. I stumbled over to the window and looked out. The interrogation room faced the street on the second story in a corner of the building. A gutter from the roof of the building went all the way down to the ground. It was still light outside.

I made a choice. I would try to escape, or I would never get out of the interrogation room alive. Somehow, I managed to squeeze my battered body through the bars of the window. Holding onto the gutter, I climbed down from the second story to the street. I ran as fast as I could. I did not know where I was going. I saw a twenty-year-old girl with a white armband walking on the street. I stopped and said to her, "Will you take me home? I escaped from the Gestapo. I need a place to hide."

"Yes. Follow me," the girl said and took me to the house

where she lived with her parents. They immediately dressed me up in women's clothes and a wig. I told them the whole story of the American money and the Gestapo interrogation. I told them that I was from Krosno. I hid in their house without leaving, dressed as a girl, for the next three weeks. While I recovered from the beatings, I learned that the money dealer's daughter had been safely released after the Gestapo obtained all my American money. I also learned that my parents were notified that I was arrested and that I had escaped. My parents did not know where I was hiding.

My mother went to work trying to pay off the Gestapo. She gave money to a cousin with connections to the Gestapo. A few days later, the cousin told my mother, "It's all done. It's all set. The Gestapo's not looking for him anymore. He can come home." After learning that my mom had paid off the Gestapo, I changed out of the women's clothes. I took the train back to Krosno.

I arrived at my house and opened the door. Baker, the murderous Gestapo man, was inside my house waiting for me. Baker knew me because he often patronized my father's tailor shop. Baker looked at me and said, "Come on, let's go."

ɞ

A PRIEST

B aker took me one block to the Gestapo office. We entered. Baker called the chief of the local Gestapo. The chief came in, looked at me, and said, "This is the guy. Why did you run away? Tell me."

"I don't know. They arrested me and I got scared, so I escaped," I said.

"You are not going to escape this time," the chief replied. He put me in handcuffs and escorted me to a car. We drove to an adjacent town called Jaslo, where there was a large political prison.

When I arrived at the prison, Nazi guards took all my belongings and made me completely undress. They sprayed me with lice disinfectant, made me take a cold shower, and then gave me thin prison clothes. I was placed in a large cell with eleven other prisoners. In the cell were twelve straw sacks to sleep on and a tiny barred window too high to see out. There was no running water or toilet, only two buckets: one for water, one to relieve yourself. I quietly lay down on an empty straw sack. My only thought was that I had to get out.

A trustee, a prisoner with special privileges, entered the cell at seven o'clock the next morning and took away the two buckets. The trustee left a fresh bucket of water, an empty bathroom bucket, and a little breakfast. The breakfast was only some black bread and a little black water that was supposed to be coffee. I ate my small portion of bread and freshened up with the water from the bucket. One of my cellmates used water from the bucket and a razor to shave anybody that wanted a shave.

Another cellmate took out a bible and read from the New Testament in Polish. I had never heard the New Testament because it is not part of the Torah. As he talked about the meaning of the passage he had just read, I realized that this prisoner was a Roman Catholic priest. The middle-aged priest put a small piece of bread in each cellmate's mouth and recited a prayer. I did not understand what was happening.

There was no radio, no television, no books, no newspapers, but the cell was big enough to move around. I did squats and sit-ups so that I was not stagnant. I told the eleven prisoners in my cell, "My name is Solomon Berger. The Gestapo arrested me. I escaped, but was recaptured." I did not confide further. My cellmates were all Polish political prisoners, mostly uneducated Polish farmers. I was the only Jew. We had all resisted the German occupation. Nobody told their personal stories. We all hoped the Germans would lose. In the afternoon, the priest read and explained a different section of the New Testament. Everybody crossed themselves, so I learned to cross myself in the same way. In the evening, we got some dinner and fresh buckets. Everyday was the same except Sundays, when we got a little marmalade that we could spread on the bread. I started to lose a lot of weight. I only had one desire: get out of prison. Survive.

Once a week, Nazi guards told everybody to line up single file and walk around the prison courtyard. The guards warned us to stay in line, not to turn our heads, and not to talk to anybody. We silently walked for fifteen minutes. This was the only time we were permitted to go outside. Once a month, we were taken to a cold communal shower. Sometimes there was soap. Once in a while, we received small packages from home, with most of the items already stolen by the trustees. My mother sent pieces of bread and fruits. We could hear Nazi guards interrogating crying prisoners. We also heard some news about the war. The Germans were winning. As the routine settled in, I continued to have only one idea: try to get out. Try to survive.

The priest continued to read from his bible every morning and afternoon. He kept telling me, "Berger, study Catholicism. If you're lucky enough to be released from this prison, you'll have a better chance surviving as a Catholic Pole."

"I'll do whatever you tell me to do," I replied. I had to be very agreeable in prison. Everyday, I listened to the sermons and lectures about Catholicism. I memorized the Lord's Prayer and the Hail Mary. The priest used pieces of bread because we did not have wafers for Communion. He used water from the bucket instead of wine. Three months later, I knew all the essential Catholic customs.

The priest told me, "Berger, you are knowledgeable enough about the Catholic religion to convert if you are ever released." I thanked him but never intended to convert.

After six months, I was called into the prison office for the first time. A Nazi officer sat behind a desk. "Are you Solomon Berger?" he asked.

"Yes."

"I'm going to read you a statement," the officer continued, "then I want you to sign it." He started to read out loud from a piece of paper: "On June 18, 1940, I was in the city of Tarnow to purchase American dollars on the black market. I was arrested for my crime by Gestapo officers at the Tarnow train station. I escaped incarceration and was recaptured in Krosno. I admit that this statement is true."

"That story is not true," I told him.

"What's not true?" the officer replied.

"I was in Tarnow," I responded. "The Gestapo arrested me, I escaped, but I was not involved in any purchase of American dollars."

"You are lying."

"I'm not lying."

"Are you going to sign it?"

"No."

"For every lie that you tell me, you are going to get twenty-five lashes over your back. Now, are you going to sign?"

"No."

"Lay over. Get over the chair." I bent over one of the chairs in the office. The Nazi officer whipped my back. "One," he said. The officer lashed me again. "Two." He reached, "twenty-five," as he counted out each lash. I took off my thin prison shirt because it was soaked in blood. "Are you going to sign it?" the Nazi asked again.

"The only thing that I'm going to sign is that I was arrested. Nothing else."

"You are lying. Get back down over the chair." The officer then lashed my naked back another twenty-five times. He again counted out the number after each lashing. I had never been lashed before. All I could think about was how much it hurt. "Are you going to sign it now?"

"No," I replied again.

The Nazi officer lashed my naked back twenty-five more times. He again asked me to sign the statement. I again refused. He lashed me another twenty-five times. After a total of one hundred lashings, he said, "If you sign, I will release you from prison. If you do not sign, you are staying here."

I had nothing to lose. I said, "I'll sign the statement, even if it's not true." I signed the statement and was escorted back to my cell. I lay face down on my straw sack and immediately passed out.

GUSTA'S GRANDFATHER

Gusta's Paternal Grandparents, Bella and Tobias Friedman

I *was sixteen when the war broke out. I evacuated Lodz with my aunt and uncle and fled east to Tarnopol because it was under Soviet control. We lived peacefully there with the rest of the family under Soviet rule.*

I joined Mina in our grandfather's two-bedroom house. We lived with our grandfather, Tobias, and took care of him in every possible way. A year before the war, Mina got married, but by the time I arrived in Tarnopol, Mina's husband had run away to join the partisans fighting rogue against the German Nazis.

My grandfather always made me feel like a queen on her throne. He was Orthodox, wore a yarmulke, and prayed with a tallis on, but he was not a fanatic. One time, he told Mina before a date with a boy, "Don't bring a girlfriend along tonight. You should want to spend time with your boyfriend alone." Mina married that boyfriend. My grandfather had a delicate face, a very delicate face. He did not have blue eyes like my father, but dark eyes that were wise. He was a smart man, a really smart man. When the Soviets came to Tarnopol, he learned to speak Russian.

My grandfather loved to look at the nighttime sky. Whenever I joined him in the chilly night air, he pointed to every star and told me its name. I have never taken astronomy, but his confidence left me with no doubt that he was correct.

In 1939, my grandfather was already retired. He had run a wholesale store that sold all kinds of materials. I was only sixteen but finished with school. There was no need for me to get a job because my grandpa had enough money. During the next two years, I just looked after my grandfather.

I was eighteen in 1941 when the Germans attacked Tarnopol. My grandfather, Mina, and I looked out our window in broad daylight and saw Polish people pointing out their Jewish neighbors to the SS. SS officers then dragged the Jews out of their houses, into the street, and shot them. My grandfather wrapped himself in his tallis and started to pray. Two SS walked into our house. Mina and I stood frozen, petrified, and crying uncontrollably. The SS saw my grandfather praying in his tallis and stopped cold in their tracks. They looked back and forth between my grandfather and my sister and me dripping with tears, our eyes like a storm. My heart stopped beating.

CHAPTER THIRTEEN

✌

TARNOPOL GHETTO

The two SS officers in our house did not say anything before turning around and leaving. I felt like someone had just taken a thousand pounds off my chest. I do not know why they did not take my grandfather like the others. God watched over my grandfather and spared his life.

Soon after the Germans arrived in Tarnopol, they forced us to leave our homes. My grandfather, Mina, and I moved from our two-bedroom house into a one-bedroom apartment in a contained area of the city, the ghetto. Once in the ghetto, SS patrolled the borders. You could not run away. All Jews were forced to wear a yellow or white armband. I took my armband off every chance I had.

Every morning, SS took Mina and me, with a lot of other young Jews, out of the ghetto to do compulsory labor. I was assigned the job of folding sheets and blankets for the German soldiers. Sometimes, when I was folding a nice blanket, a very nice blanket, I wrapped it around me and covered it with my shirt. There were so many soldiers and so many blankets that one here or there was never missed. When no one was watching, I took off my armband and snuck away. I was not afraid. If someone caught me, there was nothing more I could lose.

You live or die, but not in fear. A Polish woman I knew in Tarnopol bought the secret blanket. With the money, I bought kosher food for my grandfather. In the evening, the soldiers escorted us back to the ghetto. I was very skinny, so if I had a kosher chicken, I could just put the chicken in my shirt and go back with it to the ghetto undetected.

Our one-bedroom ghetto apartment was close to the train station. Some nights, I could hear crying from the station. I heard little children yelling and screaming as they were being forced onto a train. The little children continued wailing and crying until the train was too far away to hear. Nobody heard from those children again.

After six months, the ghetto was separated into young and old. Mina and I were taken to a work camp for young people. The old people remained in the original ghetto. When they took me away from my grandfather, I felt like all my blood was gone. Every drop of blood inside me had vanished. I felt numb. My only thoughts were about my grandfather. I wondered with horror about what would happen to him now that he was alone. The Nazis had snatched away the throne that my grandfather had built for me.

I continued folding sheets for the Germans in the work camp. Whenever I had a chance, I took off my Jewish armband and went back to the ghetto to visit my grandfather. I cheered him up and brought him food. Every time I visited him, he told me to run away, to save my life. Sometimes Mina and I heard rumors that the Nazis were going to deport Jews to be killed. When we heard a rumor, we took off our armbands, snuck back to the ghetto, and hid our grandfather in his apartment so that the Nazis could not take him away. He told us, "You must run away. You must survive."

During the next three months, my sister and I saved our grand-father several times. One day while we were both at work, we heard that the SS had taken all old people. After work, I immediately took off my Jewish armband and ran to the ghetto as fast as I could. I hoped with all my heart that my grandfather would still be there. I entered his room. His cap was the first thing I saw. The yarmulke he always wore lay on the floor. I knew he had lost his cap while being dragged out against his will. I knew I would never see him again. Nobody ever came back after the Nazis took you away. I returned crying to camp and told Mina what had happened. We both broke down. We remembered together what our grandfather always told us: you must run away. You must survive.

CHAPTER FOURTEEN

ço

SOLOMON SEES HITLER

The next morning, Nazi guards called me back to the prison office. They returned my own clothes and escorted me, skinny and weak, out of the prison to my mother waiting for me outside. I could not believe I had been unexpectedly released. I hugged my mother and went home to all my family.

I did not have to return to compulsory labor because the Gestapo had permitted my father to keep his sons at the tailor shop to work for the military service. Members of the German military service provided services and provisions for the German army. After the Germans took over Krosno, they evicted many rich Jews so that military servicemen could live for free in their large houses. The servicemen wore brown uniforms, not the grey uniforms of the German army. They did not pay my father for his tailoring, but they gave us food. Mostly cereals, bread, and, very rarely, some meat. We had enough to eat.

I slowly recovered from prison and found out that my mother had paid an intermediary to the Gestapo a large amount for my release. She had sold most of her jewelry. The murderous Gestapo were also corrupt. I tried to find out what had happened in Poland during the six months of my incarceration. Everything was upside down. The Nazis established ghettos in large Polish towns where they dehumanized Jewish people and forced them into slave labor. The Nazis forced strong young Jewish males to construct the labor camps that became killing camps where Nazis gassed Jewish people and burned them in crematoriums by the tens of thousands. Polish Catholics who resisted the Nazis were also killed by the thousands in the same way. Partisan resistance against the German occupation started to spring up all over Poland.

Thousands of Catholic Poles organized into separate partisan groups. The Polish partisans did not admit Jews into their ranks. I wanted to escape to the forest and join them as a Catholic. I told my parents and brothers about the priest in prison who taught me all about Catholicism. I assured them that I never intended to convert.

As soon as I could walk, I visited Haftel, a Jewish printer in Krosno. He printed Nazi documents and made official rubber stamps for the Gestapo. He made false identification papers with a Gestapo stamp for anybody with money. My brothers did not come with me. They were scared of being caught. I snuck into Haftel's house and exchanged my little money for a Nazi-issued Polish identification card. Name: Jan Jerzowski. Nationality: Polish. Profession: Tailor. Religion: Polish. All non-Jews in Poland were considered Polish. I hid my new identity behind a board in the attic of my house.

My father, three brothers, and I manually operated sewing machines with foot pedals to prepare German military uniforms. German uniforms were high quality in comparison to the Poles' or the Soviets'. We also did some private work for servicemen, SS, and Gestapo. They bragged, so I found out what was happening in the war. Jews still had no radios or newspapers. Nazi Germany had conquered most of Europe. Belgium, Holland, Yugoslavia, Norway, Denmark, and even France had fallen. England had resisted the German forces and was very resilient. The Germans could not cross the English Channel.

May, 1941. Germany began building large forces near the Soviet border and the River San. In early June, many Gestapo and SS accumulated in Krosno. Nazi police were on every roof in the center of town. With my white armband, I walked to Krosno's main street that went west to the airport. Nazis lined both sides of the street. I was the only Jewish person in sight standing among them. A loud voice from the west said, "Heil, Heil, Heil."

I saw four black Mercedes convertibles driving east from the airport through Krosno. Gestapo officers with machine guns sat in the first. Adolf Hitler, wearing a German army uniform, stood in the second car greeting all the people along the roadside. He had a small moustache, angry face, and swastika on his left arm. Benito Mussolini, in an ordinary Italian uniform and black cap, sat next to Hitler and did not greet the people. The Hungarian Prime Minister, Laszlo Bardossy, sat in the third convertible. Gestapo officers with machine guns filled the fourth. As Hitler drove past, I was twenty yards away from his car. I was plain ordinary scared and could not even think about attacking Hitler because the Gestapo would have killed me on the spot.

I ran back home to tell my whole family. "You are stupid," they said. "You are always doing stupid things. You create trouble for yourself." It did not bother me because I knew that I was built to be a resistant person.

Chapter Fifteen

AN EARLY WINTER

June 22, 1941. Nazi Germany heavily bombed the Soviet Union. The Soviets started to retreat as the Germans pushed eastward with tanks, artillery, and masses of soldiers. The SS followed the advancing German army, killing as many Jewish people as possible. They committed indescribable atrocities. Servicemen in the tailor shop bragged. They said that Hitler broke the nonaggression pact between Germany and the Soviet Union in the height of summer with plans to defeat the Soviets before winter. The servicemen were 100% convinced that it would not take more than three months. They were convinced that the Nazis would be the masters of the world.

The German Nazis organized themselves like a machine. They reorganized their conquered territories and nobody could beat them. The Nazis created hate. They had pride that they were born better than everybody else and that they could do what they wanted.

September, 1941. The Germans took Kiev.

November, 1941. German forces arrived at Leningrad,

Moscow, and Stalingrad. We heard that the Soviet government had escaped from Moscow. The servicemen bragged that there was not going to be a Soviet Union, only a German Nazi government all over Europe.

Then, it started to snow. Winter came early. I had just turned twenty-two. The Soviets brought out a tremendously large Siberian force that was specially trained for winter warfare and started to push the Germans back to the west. The servicemen bragged that the Germans were conducting a strategic withdrawal.

May, 1942. The Gestapo announced that all Jews in Krosno would be moved to a ghetto. They then evicted a whole block of Sienkiewicz Street in central Krosno, five minutes from my house. The SS surrounded the entire block in barbed wire, with only one entrance. The windows on the borders were boarded up so that Jewish people could not see outside the ghetto. We knew that we could not take our belongings with us when we were forced to move, so we began selling everything to Polish peasants who paid mostly in food. Nobody in my family trusted that the Nazis would let us live. They were shooting and gassing Jewish people by the tens of thousands. We thought nobody would survive. We were death row inmates waiting to be executed.

August 9, 1942. A balmy Sunday in Krosno. An announcement from the Gestapo was on every Jewish front door. It said, "You are ordered to report to the marketplace near the railroad station for registration at nine o'clock in the morning on Monday, August 10, 1942. You will leave your house unlocked and available for police inspection. You are permitted to bring one small bag per person. Anybody who is caught after nine o'clock in a house, in the street, or in hiding will be shot on sight."

Panic soon erupted in the streets of Krosno. Some people tried to escape. Most were caught and shot. Many Polish people told the Germans where Jewish people were hiding. My family all suspected a deportation on Monday morning. We had heard stories about the gas chambers. Young Jews would be put to work in the ghetto, and those who were unable to work would be deported to death camps. We could not escape or hide.

My brothers and I did not want to leave my parents and sister alone. My father was seventy-seven years old and my sister had two small children. We decided that the whole family would go together to the marketplace at nine o'clock the next morning. We made small packages to take with us. I prepared a rucksack with a change of underwear, a change of pants, a spare jacket, and extra food. My mother did not want to give her silver candelabra to the Nazis, so she took it to Mrs. Duchowski's house. Mrs. Duchowski, a good friend of my mother's, was a Catholic Pole. I played soccer with Mr. Duchowski when I was younger.

Monday, August 10, 1942. A clean and sunny day. I woke up early with the rest of my family. We all put on double underwear in case the Nazis took our bags. We ate some breakfast together and placed some extra food in our little rucksacks. At eight o'clock, I walked with my father, mother, three brothers, sister, her husband Raphael, and their two daughters to the marketplace by the railroad station.

Chapter Sixteen

೮੭

AUGUST 10, 1942

My father had a small, dark beard. He wore his regular suit with a black top hat over his yarmulke. My mother, sister Bella, and her two daughters wore their nicest dresses. Sonya was only ten but carried herself like a grown-up lady. Manya was only six-and-a-half and did not know what was going on. Everyone had an armband. Many other Jewish families were already in the marketplace. Over two thousand Jewish people had assembled. Families were all standing together. I waited with my family for nine o'clock to arrive. We all knew something bad was going to happen.

At exactly nine o'clock, trucks full of Gestapo, SS, German police, Polish police, and Ukrainian police started to arrive. They exited the trucks and surrounded the marketplace. The SS had machine guns. I did not have a weapon. Nobody could escape. The Gestapo gave orders in German to the Jewish Committee who translated them into Polish. We were ordered to line up four deep, men in different lines from women and children. We all followed the orders and lined up. There was no chaos. I stood in line with my three brothers, one behind the other. My father and Raphael stood in a line next to us. My mother, Bella, Sonya, and Manya all stood together in a different line together.

A Gestapo with a little stick in his hand then started walking around the marketplace, pointing old people out from the lines and saying, "You, come out!" A policeman escorted the chosen people into the back of a truck. If one could not get into the truck by their own power, the policeman would simply pick the old person up and throw them in. The Gestapo with the little stick approached my family. He pointed his stick at my father and said, "You, come out!" My father was the only one selected from our family.

My father grabbed my three brothers and me. He brought us close to him and said in Yiddish, "Boys, this is the end. They are going to put me on one of those trucks. Once they put me on a truck, we will never see each other again. Nobody comes back from the trips that these trucks make." My brothers and I were all crying. My father pulled his four sons closer and said, "You boys make me a promise. You must survive. Don't be a hero, just try to survive any way you can. Tell the story of what happened today and during the German occupation." A policeman grabbed my father and escorted him away from us. My father climbed into a truck full of other old Jewish people.

As we stood crying in the marketplace, five hundred old Jewish men and women were loaded into the military trucks. Several SS vehicles with machine guns mounted on top accompanied the trucks, with my father, out of the marketplace.

The Nazis ordered us to remain standing. They shot or beat to death anyone who sat down on the ground. Policemen dragged the dead bodies out of the marketplace full of crying people. We were being handled like cattle. An hour later, empty trucks drove back into the marketplace. Military servicemen exited the armed escort vehicles.

The Jewish Committee announced in Polish that the military service needed young people to work. Servicemen walked around the marketplace selecting young Jews. One approached my family and pointed at my three brothers and me. "Come out!" he shouted.

I turned to my mother and sister and said, "I hope you all survive." The serviceman escorted my brothers and me to the center of the marketplace along with six hundred other young Jews. Gestapo ordered us to form a single file line and begin walking toward the newly established ghetto. Policemen kept their guns pointed at us.

When we arrived at the ghetto's only entrance, a Gestapo officer stood next to a table with several secretaries. We had to register for a work permit. After an hour in line, I walked up to a secretary who asked, "Name?"

"Solomon Berger," I said.

"Profession?"

"I'm a tailor."

"Age?"

"Twenty-two." The secretary issued me a permit. I waited with my brothers inside the ghetto for an hour until all the young Jews had been registered. Servicemen gave us a piece of bread and some butter. This was all we had to eat that day.

"Find a place to live in the ghetto," a serviceman told us. "Rest up until tomorrow morning. Today is a free day." The whole ghetto only had two small apartment buildings and three single-family houses. My brothers and I went into an apartment building and searched for a room where we could all stay together. Each room had lots of wooden bunk beds. No mattresses, blankets, or pillows. The Nazis expected that fifteen to twenty people would share each room. My brothers and I found a room with two empty bunk beds and fifteen other guys. Friends and family stayed together. We rearranged the bunks so that there was space to sit on the wooden floor. We worried about what had happened to the rest of the people in the marketplace. Moishe, Joshua, Michael, and I wondered about what had happened to our mother, sister, brother-in-law, and nieces. We suspected our father was dead.

I lay down on my plain, wooden bunk. I used my rucksack as a pillow. I tried to sleep.

CHAPTER SEVENTEEN

༄

GHETTO LIFE

At daybreak, everybody had to get up. We gathered with the six hundred others in a street next to the ghetto's entrance. Gestapo and servicemen entered and ordered all the Jews to line up. A serviceman called out our names. When we heard our name, we had to say, "Yes, sir."

Servicemen started to assign jobs: loading and unloading military trains, construction at the airport, building and cleaning roads. While my brothers and I waited to be assigned work, I recognized a serviceman who had often patronized my father's shop. The serviceman spoke to a Gestapo officer in private before walking up to my brothers and me. "You are needed in the tailor shop. Follow me," he said. An armed Nazi guard and service-man then escorted us out of the ghetto and to our father's tailor shop. Even though we had been ordered to do tailoring work for the Nazis, we had been saved from hard manual labor. Moishe, Joshua, Michael, and I worked all day fixing and cleaning the Germans' well-made military uniforms. A serviceman provided us with some food during the day. At night, a Nazi guard escorted my brothers and me back to the ghetto.

I talked to people in different rooms in the ghetto trying to figure out what had happened to the rest of the people in the marketplace. One young Jew had hired a Catholic Pole to find out what was happening outside the ghetto. I heard the trucks that had left the marketplace full of old Jewish people went ten miles into the forest. All our elders had been shot into a previously prepared mass grave. My father was among them.

My mother, sister, and her family, along with more than a thousand other remaining Jewish people, mostly women and children, had to stay standing all day without food or water in the August heat. Nazis shot or beat to death anyone who sat on the ground. Before the end of the day, all those left in the marketplace were lined up and taken to the railroad station where they were loaded into cattle cars. The Gestapo then ordered the members of the Jewish Committee and Jewish police into the same train cars. The SS locked the doors from the outside. The train remained in the Krosno station for twenty-four hours while the Nazis loaded Jewish people from neighboring areas into the same train. The next nightfall, the train departed toward an unknown destination.

At daybreak, I reported for roll call. A Nazi guard escorted my brothers and me to the tailor shop where we worked until the guard came back for us at nighttime. In the ghetto that night, I learned that the cattle car train had traveled all night without stopping before arriving the next day at a camp called Belzec. A Gestapo officer with a bullhorn stood outside the train and said, "All out!" Nazis chased slower people out of the cattle cars with leather whips. "All men go to the right. All women and children go to the left," the bullhorn announced. "You will all get undressed and take a shower. After the shower, men will build houses, women and children will be assigned to barracks. If you Jews behave, work hard, and give us no trouble, we will permit you to live. Before the shower, you will leave your valuables at the valuables window and receive a receipt. After the shower, present your receipt for your valuables." The Jewish people had no choice but to follow the orders without resistance. SS packed people into shower rooms and locked the doors. The shower rooms were connected with rubber hoses to diesel truck engines. It took two hours to finally get the engines started. Twenty minutes later, all the Jews inside were dead from the carbon monoxide gas. People stood like columns of stone with no room to fall or to lean. Guards pulled out gold teeth from the dead bodies and then buried them in mass graves.

I had no more home and no more parents. I knew that any day, the Nazis were going to kill my brothers and me. My brothers and I continued to line up every morning in the ghetto, work in the tailor shop, and come back to the ghetto at night. Servicemen provided all the materials we needed to make and fix German uniforms. The rest of the Jews in the ghetto performed compulsory slave labor. We worked six days a week from sunrise to sunset. Sunday was our only day off.

We sold things to Catholic Poles for food or money. I accumulated American dollar bills in case I ever escaped. Most Jews sold things for food because they were only given a ration of black bread in the morning and at night. Fortunately, the military service provided some extra food for my brothers and me at the tailor shop. Also, my mother's friend, Mrs. Duchowski, would regularly bring food to my brothers and me. She also brought us blankets and pillows.

"We need thirty tailors to work at a nearby SS training camp," a Gestapo announced at role call one morning in September. A serviceman selected thirty tailors from a list, including Moishe and Michael. Joshua and I were not selected. Moishe and Michael were loaded into trucks and driven away. A Nazi guard escorted Joshua and me back to the tailor shop where we worked the whole day. That night, I learned that the Nazis had built special barracks in the SS camp to house the thirty Jewish tailors. Moishe and Michael were not coming back to the ghetto.

As Joshua and I continued working six days a week, we learned that Polish partisans were in the nearby forest. We made plans to escape into the forest and join the Polish underground fighters pretending to be Catholic Poles. Every day, we tried to get more information about the partisans' location.

The morning of December 3, 1942. On our way to the tailor shop, we noticed SS accumulating all around Krosno. Joshua and I were convinced that there would be another deportation. The SS did not come to Krosno for a friendly meeting. They were here for a reason. Joshua and I would escape to the forest before nightfall to join the partisans. We did not know their exact location, but there was no choice. There was no time to wait.

I retrieved my false identification card from the attic. I sewed thirty single American dollars into the shoulder pad of my coat. I also had some German money. Joshua said, "Solomon, it's twenty degrees below zero outside and we are in our summer clothes. We need winter clothes. We will need food until we are able to find the partisans. I'm going to go back to the ghetto for warm clothes and extra food. After I get back, we will escape together into the forest."

Joshua went back to the ghetto. I anxiously waited in the tailor shop for the entire day. Before nightfall, I knew Joshua was not coming back.

CHAPTER EIGHTEEN

❧

MRS. D.

There was no more time to wait. I only had a few minutes before the Nazi guard would arrive to escort me back to the ghetto. I slipped out of the tailor shop. It was too late to look for the partisans in the snow-covered forest. I carefully walked five minutes to Mrs. Duchowski's house. I knocked on her door. I hoped that she would not turn me over to the SS. Mrs. Duchowski opened the door. "The ghetto is surrounded and going to be liquidated," I said. "I need a place to hide for the next few days."

Mrs. Duchowski took me to her attic. She gave me a blanket to cover myself and some food. She said, "Wait here overnight until we see what happens." The next morning, she came back and said, "The minute it became light outside, Gestapo, SS, and police entered the ghetto. Jewish people were shot in the streets. The Nazis loaded everybody left in the ghetto into trucks and took them away."

"I have a false Christian identification card that says my name is Jan Jerzowski," I told her. "I am going to escape into the forest to join the Polish partisans. Can I remain hiding here until it is safe?"

"I have a better idea," she responded. "My husband is in charge of rebuilding a bridge on the Dniester River near the city of Stanislawow in a village called Niznow. He knows you. Take his address." Mrs. Duchowski handed me a piece of paper. "Just remember it. Don't keep this paper," she said. "Remain hiding here until the Gestapo and SS leave. Then take the train. Get to my husband. Tell him that I sent you. Tell him that you have a Christian identification card."

"Thank you," I said. It sounded like a good idea. "I will do it," I told her. She left the attic and I covered myself with her blanket. I memorized Mr. Duchowski's address.

Later that day, she said, "The Gestapo and SS took close to five hundred young Jews from the ghetto to the adjacent forest where they were all shot in front of a previously prepared mass grave." My brother Joshua was most likely caught and among them. "SS are going through every room and niche in the ghetto. They are searching for anybody still hiding," she said. I hid under her blanket hoping that the Nazis would not search Polish houses.

Two days later, Mrs. Duchowski came up and said, "The Gestapo have decided that nobody remains in the ghetto and have ordered it dismantled. They announced that there are no more Jews in Krosno." After another day, she told me, "The Gestapo and SS have all left. I will take you to the railroad station in Iwonicz tonight." Iwonicz was the next small village over on the train route to Stanislawow. I might be recognized at the Krosno station. There were no police in the small village of Iwonicz.

In the middle of the night, Mrs. Duchowski came into the attic and said, "Get your Polish identification card. Let's go!"

I followed her out of the house into the snow. We walked five miles southeast through snowfields for two hours to the village of Iwonicz.

Behind a building, I gave Mrs. Duchowski some of my German money and said, "I will wait here. You buy me the ticket." She walked alone to the train station, purchased my ticket, and walked back.

"Good luck," she said. We said goodbye to each other and she left. I waited behind the building for an hour for the train to arrive. It was still nighttime when I boarded the train and sat down in an empty seat among Poles and Ukrainians. My shoes and socks were soaked through from the snow. My name was Jan Jerzowski.

The train traveled southeast through the night and into the next day. About halfway to Stanislawow, the train stopped for six hours in a town called Drohobych. I exited the train and walked through the streets of Drohobych for the first time. My shoes and socks were still wet. I looked for a Jewish person who could take me someplace to rest for a few hours. I saw a young man with a Star of David on his white armband. He was a little taller than me but looked about my age. I asked, "Is there a ghetto here in Drohobych?"

"Yes, we still have a ghetto," he responded.

"Are you free to go in and out?"

"We can still go in and out. It is not locked up."

"Will you take me there?" I asked him.

"Follow me."

I walked behind him to the Drohobych ghetto. We went inside an apartment building full of bunk beds. Most Jews were out working for the day. I took off my shoes and socks to dry. People gave me food and let me rest. After four hours, my socks and shoes were almost dry. I said to the young Jewish man, "It's time to catch my train."

"Follow me back to the station," he said. When we arrived, I thanked him and said goodbye. "You are going to survive the war," he told me.

"Why would you say that?" I asked.

"Because if I didn't recognize you as Jewish, nobody else will." With that, the young man left. As I waited to board the train towards Stanislawow, I felt encouragement from his words. I could survive as a Catholic. I boarded the train and began traveling southeast towards Stanislawow.

After an hour, two Ukrainian policemen boarded the train. The policemen walked down the train asking the passengers for identification. A policeman approached. I remained calm as I handed my Polish identification card to him.

Chapter Nineteen

MR. D.

The policeman looked at my identification card. "If you are Catholic," he said, "recite The Lord's Prayer."

Without hesitation, I said, "Our Father, who art in heaven, hallowed be thy name. Thy kingdom come, thy will be done, on earth as it is in heaven. Give us this day, our daily bread, and forgive us our trespasses as we forgive those who trespass against us. And lead us not into temptation, but deliver us from evil. Amen." The policeman handed back my card and continued walking down the aisle.

The train stopped in Stanislawow in the middle of the day. Compared to Krosno, Stanislawow was a big town of ninety thousand. The train could not go farther because the bridge across the Dniester River was demolished. I hitched a ride on a horse and buggy from the station with some fellow passengers. I got off the buggy ten miles southeast of Stanislawow near Mr. Duchowski's address in Niznow, a village of only five hundred. I waited near his house until he came home. Tadeusz Duchowski was ten years older than me and had often patronized my father's tailor shop. He had been a top Polish soccer player before the war.

We made eye contact. He recognized me. It was before sunset. Mr. Duchowski opened his door and gestured me in. Quickly, he closed the door behind me. He asked, "How did you find me here?"

"Your wife gave me your address," I said. "I have Polish identification papers. Can you help me?" I handed my false identification card to Mr. Duchowski.

He looked it over and said, "I know it's dangerous, I don't know what I can do, but I'm going to do my best."

"Thank you, thank you," I gratefully said.

"I am in charge of rebuilding the demolished train bridge over the Dniester River," he told me. "I can hire you as a Catholic Pole. Your name is Jan Jerzowski. I cannot pay you because my company cannot know."

"I have my own money," I said. "What job will I have on the bridge?"

"Your job is to make sure nobody suspects you are Jewish," he responded. "Don't eat poppy seeds. And don't use cubed sugar in your coffee. You can spend the night here. Tomorrow, I will help you find a place to live."

The next morning, he took me to the Ukrainian police station. In German-occupied territory, every resident had to register with the local police. Mr. Duchowski said to a policeman, "This is Jan Jerzowski. He was sent from western Poland to work on the bridge." Mr. Duchowski handed the policeman my identification.

The policeman wrote "Jan Jerzowski" in a ledger, handed back my card, and asked, "Jan, where are you living?"

"I am currently looking for a place to live," I responded.

"Ok. Please come back when you have an address," he said. "I will put you under Tadeusz Duchowski's address for now."

Next stop was Mr. Duchowski's construction office, located in a private house next to the river and bridge. The mother of a Polish family living in the house cooked breakfast for a group of construction workers. Everybody was paying for food. Mr. Duchowski announced, "This is Jan Jerzowski. He was sent here from western Poland to supervise the bridge construction." I looked around pretending to be a big shot. "Jan needs a place to live."

"I know somebody with an empty room," one worker said. "Jan, follow me and I will take you to him." I followed the worker out of the office toward the construction site. He introduced me to another Polish worker in his mid-thirties who lived alone and had the extra room to rent for pennies. We walked to his three-bedroom house.

My new landlord thought that I was a big man at the bridge and that he could get some benefits by treating me well. We were both happy to have company. He left me to settle in. I had never lived in a house with a shower. My room was plain and I did not have anything to put in it. I ripped out my thirty American bills from my coat's shoulder pad. I took out a single dollar and hid the rest. I went back to the police station and registered my new address. I walked around Niznow until I found a person who could exchange my American dollar for local money, Nazi-issued occupation marks. I soon found someone who wanted to exchange occupation marks for an American dollar.

I walked back to the construction office and purchased a meal. At the construction site, thirty people were rebuilding the steel train bridge. It was cold outside, but the river was too big to freeze. The Dniester ran through Poland and Romania into the Black Sea. Little boats traveled up and down. As the foreman, I just watched everyone else work on the bridge. Nobody questioned me.

Days in December were short. By four o'clock, everyone finished working and went back to the office to get paid. I went back to my room and hoped that the workers would assume I had already been paid. That night, I talked to my landlord, trying to learn what was going on locally. He said, "The Germans are forcing most local people to go back to Germany for compulsory labor. Many have escaped and established partisan groups. They are fighting against the Germans from caves in the forests. Nazis are hunting them but don't know their way around our large forest lands." He asked about me.

"I am a Polish patriot," I said. "I came from western Poland to supervise the bridge construction."

I woke up the next morning at seven o'clock and walked to church for mass just after sunrise. I wanted to be known as a good Catholic. I listened to the priest give a sermon for half an hour. I walked to the construction office for some breakfast and asked the secretary for a folder, notebook, and pen. That day, I walked around the construction site taking pretend notes. I did not know anything about building a bridge. The Polish workers all worked hard on rebuilding the steel train bridge and did not question me. Every move I made, I was careful not to be recognized as a Jew. I was lucky to speak Polish without a Jewish accent because Polish people could recognize a Jew from a mile away. Polish Catholics were taught to be anti-Semitic. If anyone found out that I was Jewish, I would be killed.

Everyday, I went to church in the morning, the office for breakfast, and then pretended to be a supervisor at the construction site all day. Every three or four days, I exchanged another American dollar for occupation marks. After a few days, the priest approached me after morning mass. He asked, "When is your next confession?"

"I just confessed in another village," I replied. I did not want to confess because the priest might figure out that I was a Jew. I told him that I was a Polish patriot from western Poland. The priest told me that he was also a Polish patriot. Most of the Poles in Niznow were Polish patriots. They wanted Poland to regain its independence from Nazi Germany.

In church, I met an unmarried Polish schoolteacher named Christina who was also a Polish patriot. She had blonde hair and was ten years older than me. She called me Jashu. Christina went to church everyday because the Germans had closed the schools. After a couple weeks, Christina took me to her house and introduced me to her family. Sometimes, they invited me over for dinner. I liked Christina, but I did not intend to make a love affair of it. As Christina and I spent more time together, I had to be very careful not to become too involved. Polish Catholics were not circumcised.

On Christmas Eve, the Polish construction workers met at a house to celebrate. At midnight, the Poles broke bread and greeted each other in a certain way. I had never celebrated Christmas. My eagle eyes watched the others to imitate what they were doing. On Christmas day, we had a big feast and took communion at the local church. The priest put a wafer in my mouth. I said the prayers just like everyone else.

I wrote a letter to my brothers at the SS camp near Krosno, telling them that I had survived. A construction worker sent it from another town. I hoped Michael and Moishe were still alive to read my letter.

Late January, 1943. The Germans lost the Battle of Stalingrad. It was the first major German defeat. Three hundred thousand German soldiers were killed or taken prisoner by the Red Army in Stalingrad alone. Everyone in Niznow knew because we still had unrestricted access to newspapers and radios. As the bridge neared completion, I made contacts with local partisans who snuck into town for provisions. At church, the priest kept asking me to confess and I kept telling him, "I confessed in the neighboring village. I will confess again soon."

In February, all local people in Niznow had to report to the Gestapo with their birth certificates to receive internal passports. Without an internal passport, I would be arrested. I told Christina that I could not go home to western Poland to get my birth certificate because the Gestapo were looking for me. She said that the local priest could issue a birth certificate, so we walked to the church. She convinced the priest that I was a good Polish patriot who had escaped the Gestapo and needed a birth certificate. The priest sympathized and issued me a birth certificate. Name: Jan Jerzowski. Parents: Marion and Rosa Jerzowski. Born: Krakow, October 28, 1919. In very small letters at the bottom of the certificate, the priest wrote in Polish, "This birth certificate was issued by verbal testimony."

I went alone to the Gestapo with my birth certificate. I had to make decisions on the spot. Nothing was planned. As I waited in line, I thought, "How am I going to get away with this?" I then presented my birth certificate to a Gestapo. I could tell that he could not read the small Polish writing at the bottom. He issued me a passport with the name Jan Jerzowski.

One month later, the bridge was completed. Mr. Duchowski took me aside and said, "My company is leaving. We are going to be under the supervision of the SS. You can't come with us. You need to find your own way. Make me a promise: if you get caught, please say I knew nothing." Mr. Duchowski knew anyone hiding a Jewish person would be treated like a Jew.

I promised and thanked him for his help. He left Niznow the next day. I remained with my landlord. Two days later, the labor department announced that the bridge was completed so all workers had to report to the labor department to register for work in Germany. Some workers prepared to go while most said, "We are not going into Germany to work for the Nazis. They will lose the war. We are going to escape to the forest and join the partisans." I would escape to the forest with them. My few remaining American dollars would be worthless in the forest, so I purchased a .38 handgun and a rifle from a Polish man who had buried his weapons before the Germans took over.

In the middle of the night, I went to Christina's house. "I have to go," I told her. "Thank you for all your help." I left and met up with twenty Polish construction workers near the bridge. Most had firearms, and some had grenades. All of our arms were left over from World War I. We snuck out of Niznow and into the forest.

✧

Chapter Twenty

ESCAPE ON A TRAIN

*S*oon there were rumors that SS were forcing all Jews onto trains
for deportation to death camps. Mina and I followed our grandfather's advice to escape the Nazis and flee from Tarnopol. They
wanted to murder us all.

*A friendly German officer approached Mina and said, "In two
days, a transport of Russian women will pass through Tarnopol on
its way to Germany, where they will work on farms. You should join
this transport and escape deportation."*

*Mina fled the work camp first. She boarded a train full of Rus-
sian women. I prayed that Mina's Russian was better than mine. I
planned to leave a few days later on a second train. Mina and I did
not escape together because we would be suspected of being Jewish
sisters trying to escape. If a Nazi hit her, I would have screamed
and exposed us.*

*I disappeared from the work camp in Tarnopol two days after
Mina. I only brought the two shirts, undershirt, and underwear
that I was wearing as I walked to the train station. My only thought*

*was, "I must survive like my grandfather told me." The train sta-
tion was full of Polish women. I blended in with the crowd and had
no problem boarding when the train arrived. Nobody had tickets.
The Polish women were traveling to Germany to earn money working for the Germans.*

*I wondered what I would say if I was caught without Polish iden-
tification papers. Out of nowhere, an answer came into my mind. I
would say, "Somebody stole my baggage with all my papers. My name
is Stanislava Urbanska. I want to work in Germany." I did not go
to a judge to change my name. I just changed it myself in a second.
The hardest part was to remember it.*

*As the train traveled westward across the war-torn Polish coun-
tryside, I started to talk to the other passengers. I learned where they
came from and where they were going in Germany. Everything was
going fine until we reached the German border. The train stopped.
Everybody had to leave the train for border inspection. I hid in a
bathroom because I was not on the transportation list. I wanted
to be a little mouse that could hide in a hole and never be found.
There was nowhere to hide in the tiny bathroom. Two Gestapo
opened the bathroom door.*

"I bet you she is Jewish," one said to the other.

*The other responded, "No, she doesn't look Jewish. She looks like
a German."*

They took me off the train and asked me, "What is your name?"

"Stanislava Urbanska," I said.

*"Where are you from?" I told the Gestapo that I was from a city
in Russia that the Soviets had taken back from the Germans. The
Gestapo responded, "You're not on our transportation list. Where are
your papers?"*

"My baggage, with all my papers, was stolen," I said. "I don't have anything. Everything was stolen."

"Why are you here?" the Gestapo asked me.

"I want to work in Germany, so they put me on this train."

"Why didn't you register?"

"If I registered, they would separate me from my friends," I told them. The Gestapo asked me repeatedly if I had any Jewish friends or connections to the Jews. "No," I kept responding. If I had said yes, they would have shot me beside the train.

***

CHAPTER TWENTY-ONE

A VIVID DREAM

*T*he Gestapo took me to a prison back in Poland. My escape plan
had failed.

When I arrived, guards ordered me to take off my clothes and
take a shower. When I heard the word "shower," I instantly cried. I
remembered what people had told me about Jewish people going into
showers and not coming out. "We have to disinfect you," a guard said.

I thought it was the last day of my life until I saw Polish people
coming out of the shower. I still did not want to take a shower so I
said, "But I'm clean. I don't have lice."

"No, honey," the guard responded, "we have to disinfect you.
Take off your clothes." I took off my clothes and entered the shower.
Water came out instead of poison. After the shower, I was put into a
cell with one hundred and sixty other Polish women. The walls were
made of stone and the hard floors were cold. Wooden barrack bunk
beds had no mattresses or blankets. Luckily, it was the summer.

I learned that the other inmates were Polish political prisoners.
Unlike everyone else, I was happy to be in prison. My story had

fooled the Nazis. The first night, while I listened to the breathing of the other prisoners, I closed my eyes and said to myself, "Stanislava Urbanska, Stanislava Urbanska, Stanislava Urbanska."

The prisoners prayed everyday, so I began to learn their Polish prayers about Jesus. Whatever they said, I said. Whatever they did, I did. I had to be a Catholic, or I would be killed. I quickly learned. Every morning, guards came into the cell for a head count. I tried to hide behind a tall person because I was afraid someone would recognize me.

During the daytime, I was taken to the launderette where I washed, dried, and ironed German soldiers' clothes and sheets. I took a shower and had clean clothes to wear everyday. The launderette was adjacent to the interrogation room. Sometimes, when I was folding the soldiers' clothes, I could hear Nazi interrogations of political prisoners. When a prisoner did not want to admit something, the Gestapo took pliers to their nails.

One ugly Gestapo woman looked liked a devil. I was so petrified of her devilish face that it burned into my memory. Everyday, she took me and several other prisoners to and from the cell and the launderette. I always did the best work I knew how. The Gestapo woman brought me food and wanted me to get free so I could baby-sit for her sister's children. I prayed to God to stay in prison so that I would not have to work for her family.

One morning, a Gestapo called me forward. My heart stopped beating. Had someone recognized me? Were any of the prisoners from Tarnopol? Or Stefke? Everybody watched as the guards led me to the interrogation room. In the room, the Gestapo asked me over and over if I knew any Jews. Somehow, I remained calm and stuck to my story. It was either lie and live, or tell the truth and die. I did not want to leave prison because I had no place to go. Even if I had a place to go, I had no money to get there. Even if I had money and a place to go, someone on the outside could recognize me as a Jew. In prison, everybody thought that I was a Catholic Pole.

Prisoners shared packages from home with extra food, so I was never hungry. The guard who watched us at night was very nice to me. My pleasant prison routine continued until I got so sick that I could not talk or even swallow water without extreme pain. I continued working and did not tell anybody. One day I was too sick to work, so I hid under my bed. A nurse was sent to examine me and said, "Scarlet fever." If I did not die today, I would die tomorrow. There was nothing to lose, so there was no reason to be afraid.

I recovered after a week, but other prisoners with scarlet fever were not so fortunate. One night, after six months in political prison, I had a dream. I was walking side by side with my grandfather in a beautiful garden. Fruit trees sparkled in the midday sunlight. The sun shone on both of us. We were free. I wanted to hug and kiss my grandfather as we walked in the warm sun. My grandfather said to me, "You have to get out of here. You have to live." Standing in the garden sun with my grandfather felt so good that I woke up.

I saw the cell around me and felt very low. I sensed my grandfather's spirit watching over me, trying to tell me something. I kept thinking about my dream but had nobody to share it with. I said to myself, "Everything was just a dream and nothing else."

Three days after the dream, I was at work doing laundry when a guard called out, "Stanislava Urbanska! Come here!" I felt like a knife had cut off my legs. I could not move. I was nailed down to the floor but had to react fast. I could not show my fear.

"Can I go to the bathroom first?" I asked. The guard let me go *and I pulled myself together. After splashing cold water on my face, I calmly returned to the guard. We walked through a beautiful garden with fruit trees and the sun was shining just like in my dream. It was warm outside, but inside I was cold. We walked to an office at the end of the garden. Inside, the officer in charge was eating his lunch. He turned to look at me and offered me some food. I said, "Thank you. I'm not hungry."*

"You look better in prison than a lot of people do outside," the officer said. I told him that I would gladly trade places with anybody on the outside. He opened my file and looked it over. He did not ask me anything. "Take her back," the Gestapo officer ordered the guard.

"How much longer am I going to be here?" I asked the officer.

"A couple more days."

"I don't believe you," I responded. The guard then escorted me back to my cell. A few days later, they released me from prison. I was free on the outside, but inside I was very lonely. Would I ever see Mina again? Would I have to hide my real identity forever? Where would I go? I had become friends with another prisoner named Maria whose husband had run away with the partisans. In retaliation, the Nazis had locked Maria in prison even though she had a six-week-old baby. Maria's sister took care of her baby and lived in Katowice, the same town as the prison. Maria's sister avoided prison because her husband joined the German army. After filing divorce papers from prison, Maria had been released a week before me. She came to pick me up and took me to her sister's house. I said, "Can I have some water," and fainted for the first time in my life.

Maria told her sister that I had nowhere to go. Maria's sister let me live in the house with her two small children and her father-in-law. The father-in-law often said, "When you are older, and my son comes back from the army, you will be my daughter-in-law." He did not know that I was Jewish. Everyone thought I was a Polish girl. The father-in-law was wonderful to me when he was sober, but terrible when drunk. When he drank, he cursed about the Jews.

I continued to work in the same launderette where I had worked while in prison. Everyday, I went to the launderette and washed the Germans' sheets. When I gave clean sheets to the soldiers, I was not supposed to talk to them. Often times Maria's sister asked me, "Why don't you go out and meet boys?"

"I already went to jail once. I don't want to go a second time," I told her. "I am waiting until the war ends. You go have a good time and I will baby-sit."

I stayed with Maria's family. We talked about how the Germans were losing. All my old friends were gone. My family was gone. I just wanted to live to see the Germans break down. That was all I was living for.

Chapter Twenty-Two

co

THE PARTISANS

We walked deeper into the forest. We knew the Polish partisans had lookouts on patrol. There were also Russian partisan groups farther to the east. It was March, and the snow was almost gone. Two miles into the forest, Polish partisan lookout patrolmen stopped us. Two partisans about my age escorted us to their commander. We followed them deeper until we reached an area with many caves dug into the ground.

The lookout patrol took us to a Polish man in his mid-thirties. A worker in my group said to the commander, "We just escaped from the Germans. We want to join you."

"You are welcome," the commander responded. The partisans wanted to recruit as many people as possible to help fight the Germans. A partisan led me to a warm cave tunneled under the snow to get some rest. In the morning, I saw fifty other partisans emerge from nearby caves. There were a total of two hundred in our group. We spread out over the forest so the Germans would never find us all at once. We were eighty-five percent men, with no children or old people. Women kept house while men performed lookout patrols, disrupted German transports, or traveled to villages for supplies. During the day, we stayed in caves or camouflaged in trees. I learned to look for moss on the north side of trees for directions in the forest. Some nights, the commander selected a small group of men to sabotage German supply lines. A few days after my arrival in the forest, the commander selected me and five other men to put a landmine under a highway.

I followed the other five guys through the forest with my handgun on my side and my rifle in my hands. I kept thinking about my father's words: "Don't be a hero, just try to survive any way you can." We walked to a dirt highway, dug a hole in the road, placed a mine inside, covered it with earth, and went back into the forest to wait. Two hours later, we heard a large explosion. We snuck back to the highway and observed from behind the trees. We had blown up a German supply truck. Two partisans left the cover of the forest to inspect. They came back and said that there were no survivors. We ran to the highway, grabbed any weapons and food that had survived the blast, and ran back into the forest.

Over the next fourteen months, I went along with small groups at night to place landmines on highways and railroad tracks. If there were a lot of Germans left alive after an explosion, we could not bring back supplies. Sometimes, if there were only a few Germans alive, certain partisans left the forest to shoot them so that we could get the supplies. The rest of us just fired into the air to make noise. My groups avoided detection and attack.

When possible, we left the forests to go into villages under the cover of nightfall. The local Polish villagers supported us with food and information. They let us know right away whenever the Germans accumulated forces to attack us. We would then go deeper into the forest where the Germans did not follow.

About fifty miles east of my Polish partisan group was a very large group of partisans under the command of a Russian general called Kopac. There were thousands of Russian partisans under Kopac's command. In general, they did not like the Poles. They did not like the Jews either.

My co-partisans called me Jashu. I pretended to speak only a little German like other Catholic Poles. When we went to the river to wash up, I never took off my shorts. No one ever suspected that I was Jewish. The partisans drank smelly homemade vodka everyday like water. I drank tall glasses to fit in and then snuck away and forced myself to throw up, so I could function. Drunk partisans would always say, "The Germans are losing. The war is coming to an end, but we have to thank Hitler for getting rid of the Jews for us."

One day, the commander ordered me to Stanislawow to get information because I spoke better German than the other partisans. He said that a beggar would be sitting near the train station exit in Stanislawow. I had to say to the beggar, "Hitler has a nice day today."

The beggar would then answer, "I agree with that completely." After successfully exchanging passwords, he would tell me some important information. The commander gave me a work order forged by a different partisan. The work order said in Ukrainian that I was to report to the labor department in Stanislawow for work in Germany. I walked alone to a small village where I purchased a train ticket to Stanislawow. I boarded the train and traveled a few stops.

When the train stopped in Stanislawow, a Gestapo with a bull-horn announced in German, "Everybody will exit the train through the front door. Have your documents ready." The announcement was then translated into Ukrainian. I lined up with the other passengers and made my way toward the front of the train.

I stepped out of the train and saw SS and policemen lining both sides of my path. My heart raced as I clutched my Nazi-issued passport and forged work order. I walked through the line and up to a Gestapo and Ukrainian policeman. The Gestapo asked in German, "Why did you come here?"

I pretended that I did not know any German. The Gestapo knew Poles could not speak German. I said in Polish, "I don't understand what you're asking me."

"What did you come here for?" the Gestapo asked again in German.

"I don't understand any German," I said in Polish.

"He is asking you why you came to town," the Ukrainian policeman then said in Polish.

"I have an order to report to the labor department for work in Germany," I answered in Polish. I handed my documents to the Gestapo, who pretended to read my passport and work order, but was looking in my eyes the whole time. I looked straight back into his eyes. My heart beat outside of my chest. The Gestapo handed me back my documents.

"Forward," he said in German. I remained standing still looking at the Gestapo until the policeman told me to move along in Polish. I walked out of the train station and saw a young male beggar sitting on the ground next to the exit.

I approached the beggar and said, "Hitler has a nice day today."

"I agree with that completely," the beggar responded. He gestured for me to come closer and quietly said, "There will be a conference with the SS and Gestapo leaders in town today. The Nazis suspect the Ukrainians are going to revolt. Germany promised the Ukrainians independence after winning the war. The Ukrainians are preparing to revolt because they know Germany will never give them independence."

I walked alone into town, leaving the beggar at the train station. I walked around Stanislawow and then went back to the station. I took the next train back to the partisans and told my commander what the beggar had said.

In early April of 1944, I was already twenty-four. The Germans retreated from the areas near the forests. The Soviet attack advanced to the west. I would leave the forest with half a dozen others. We would try to take Niznow because the Nazis had retreated. We wanted to arrive in Niznow before the Soviets so we could get more supplies. Although the Germans were gone, a Hungarian regiment was still stationed in Niznow. Only a few Germans commanded the entire Hungarian regiment. We thought the Hungarians would not bother us.

As soon as my group entered Niznow, five hundred Hungarian soldiers surrounded us in the street. We lay down our weapons and put our hands up. The Hungarians lined us up and marched us into a prison cell. A Hungarian soldier told us, "You will all be executed at midnight."

Two Germans remained guarding the cell door. I silently waited in the prison cell with the other captured partisans. My only thought was, "This is it. This is it."

Chapter Twenty-Three

ℭℜ

THE RED ARMY

Hungarians killed the German guards in the middle of the night. A Hungarian soldier opened the cell door and said, "Get lost!" The partisans and I were all in shock. We could not believe we had been saved. The Hungarian soldier yelled, "You better get going!"

Most partisans in my group were local and went home. I lay down on the ground in the street because I had nowhere to go. An hour later, the Red Army entered Niznow. I watched as the Hungarian soldiers lay down their arms. The Soviets marched the Hungarians into the same prison from which they had just released me.

The Soviets did not bother me so I stayed in Niznow, sleeping on the ground. I followed Soviet soldiers into houses where they ordered the villagers to give us food. The Red Army advanced through Niznow, pushing the Germans back. After a week, the Germans reorganized and launched a counteroffensive. The Soviets retreated.

I discarded my arms in Niznow and went east with the Red Army as a civilian. They killed any civilian who had a weapon. We retreated southeast for two days, hitching rides on buggies. The German army was sixty miles away. We heard loud artillery firing. The Germans could fire artillery up to fifty miles. We picked up our pace.

I was in the middle of an open field when planes started to dive at me with machine guns. Bombs blasted all over the field. There was no place to take cover. It was April. Nothing was growing in the field after the frozen winter. Soviet soldiers dug ditches with their helmets. I dug with my hands as fast as possible. As I burrowed my head and body into the ground, a bomb crashed near me. German planes dove down with machine guns: puh, puh, puh, puh, puh, puh, puh, puh. I looked from side to side. The planes circled around the sky and dove down again. Dead people lay all around the field.

"Am I going to get out alive?" I asked myself. "Is Germany still that strong?" Bombs and bullets rained down on the open field for half an hour. German planes flew back to the west. I stood up without a scratch. Looking at all the dead, I thought, "I'm alive. I'm alive."

I continued retreating southeast through Bukovina and into Romania. The Soviets finally stopped retreating after crossing the River Prut and entering Chernivtsi, a town of one hundred thousand people and a large Soviet force already established. I slept in houses or on the ground in Chernivtsi amongst other partisans and civilians. The Soviet and German armies started to reorganize. The River Prut separated them.

After two weeks in Chernivtsi, the Soviets established a draft of all young people over the age of eighteen. A Soviet soldier grabbed me off the street and escorted me to the draft board. A different soldier gave me a short questionnaire to fill out that asked for name, age, nationality, education, profession, and languages spoken.

I wrote, "Jan Jerzowski, 24, Catholic Pole, elementary school, tailor, and Polish, German, some Russian." The partisans had taught me some Russian in the forest. I handed the questionnaire to the Soviet draft board officer. He briefly reviewed my form, filled out some military papers, and handed me a document stating that my name was, "Ivan Marianowicz Jerzowski."

He said, "Ivan Marianowicz, you are now in the Red Army. You will start training." With my new name, I followed several other newly-inducted Soviet soldiers to the army barracks in houses that the Red Army had taken over. We were assigned an empty bed, given a locker, training clothes, and a plain Soviet uniform. My platoon consisted of one hundred and fifty Polish, Ukrainian, Romanian, and Russian soldiers. We all had to follow the orders of the Soviet officer who commanded our platoon.

In the morning, my platoon washed up, put on our training clothes, and ate a breakfast of raw herrings with lots of dry garlic. After breakfast, a Soviet officer instructed us for two hours on how to handle arms and march around in formations. Marching around seemed like a waste of time, but I followed orders. In the afternoon, we went to a classroom where we learned Russian for three hours. The rest of the day, I walked around the town talking to people and improving my Russian. Five days a week, we did the same thing.

After two weeks of the training, I was assigned guard duty. The Soviets had lookout guards twenty-four hours a day. My platoon took turns standing guard when we were not training or in class. For the next three months, I continued to live in the barracks, train with the Red Army, and stand guard. The Soviets were accumulating large forces in preparation for an offensive against Germany. In my free time, I talked with civilians to practice my Russian.

In my platoon, we all wanted the war to stop. We all just wanted to go back to our homes. Just like the Polish partisans, all the Soviet soldiers drank a lot of vodka. I started to carry around a bottle of vodka to fit in with the rest of my platoon. I drank a little but did not like it. We also ate a lot of Spam from America with bread. The cans said, "San Francisco." We did not need to cook, we just ate everything with a lot of dry garlic to keep away sickness. We always had garlic breath.

The middle of July, 1944. I heard loud artillery firing. My platoon was ordered to be ready to march. The Soviets fired sixteen rockets at a time for twenty-four hours straight. I thought I would go deaf. When the rockets finally stopped, there was not a German in sight.

Thousands of soldiers were being sent to the frontlines and getting killed right away. I saw that all the former partisans were the first being sent to the front. It was only a matter of time before my platoon was selected.

I took a chance. I went to the POW camp and found an unconscious German prisoner with a gold watch. I snuck into the cell and took the gold watch without a struggle. I was happy to see it was a Tissot because Russians especially loved Swiss watches. I put the watch on my own wrist, left the prisoner camp, and walked to the command center. An injured Soviet high-ranking officer usually ran the command centers established in new Soviet territories. I walked into the Chernivtsi command center. A Russian commanding officer in his sixties sat in the office by himself. I showed him my wrist with the Tissot and said in Russian, "Do you like my watch?"

"Of course I like your watch," the commanding officer replied.

"Let's make a deal," I responded. "I stay away from the frontline and you take the watch."

"Let me see it," he said. I took the Tissot off my wrist and handed it to the officer. I noticed that he immediately liked that it was gold. The officer put the watch to his ear to make sure it worked. The officer said, "You are going to take a class to learn how to be a translator. When you come back, I will give you a commission. The two of us will be just fine." I went back to my locker, took all my belongings, and reported back to the command center. I was given a bed in the officers' barracks.

The next day, I began my training to become a supply officer and interrogation translator. The Soviets kept me busy. I recorded the supplies that came in and out of the supply warehouse. There was not much to learn. The frontline constantly needed food and ammunition. I only had to keep records. Other soldiers unloaded the supplies from trucks and loaded the supplies into courier trucks heading to the front. When I was not working in the supply warehouse, I trained to become an interrogation translator. Soviet secret police, the NKVD, taught me the phrases I would need to translate interrogations of German prisoners.

The Soviets pushed forward for the next two weeks. Frontline soldiers continued to be brought back in body bags. I remained safely in Chernivtsi waiting for the war to end. A month later, I finished the translation class and received the rank of one-star lieutenant, the lowest ranking officer. The Red Army gave me a new uniform and a black cap with a big red star. I tailored my new uniform so that it fit perfectly.

September, 1944. The Red Army began their next offensive. The Soviets pushed forward and started to bring lots of prisoners back to Chernivtsi, mostly German officers. I was assigned to translate for a special group of NKVD. During interrogations, I sat between one NKVD officer and a German prisoner. The NKVD were professionals. They asked about special arms and operations. The German prisoners usually cooperated because they knew they could be sent to Siberia where they would never get out alive.

Only one thought repeated over and over again, "I've got to survive. I've got to survive. I've got to survive."

As the frontline pushed forward, I stayed fifty miles behind it with the NKVD interrogation officers and supplies. We marched for about three weeks until the Red Army remarkably stopped in my hometown of Krosno. The Germans were on one side of the River Wislok and the Soviets were on the other. I remained about fifty miles to the east. In November, the Soviets began pushing the Germans back and did not stop this time.

April, 1945. The Soviets were in Germany. The war was coming to an end. I took a four-week leave from the Red Army to see whether any of my family had survived.

CHAPTER TWENTY-FOUR

൪ഽ

DOUBLE AGENT

Still in my tailored Soviet uniform, I hitchhiked fifty miles to Krosno on a military truck. I walked up to the Duchowskis' house and knocked on their door. Mr. Duchowski opened it and said, "Did you have to become a Red?"

"Everything I have done was to survive," I said. "I am not a Red." Mr. Duchowski welcomed me into his house. Mrs. Duchowski came out of her room holding my mother's silver candelabra.

"Your mother gave me this to hold," she said. "I want you to have it."

"No, my mother gave it to you. You have it," I said. I was very happy to give her the silver candelabra. The only thing I wanted was pictures of my family. "Did she give you any pictures?" Mrs. Duchowski said that a Polish tailor who used to work in my father's tailor shop might have some. She told me where to find him. "Did any Jews survive in Krosno?" I asked them.

"Two dozen Jewish people survived in hiding," Mr. Duch-owski said. "They are all living together in an apartment building in the center of town."

I walked to the Polish tailor's house. To my surprise, he handed me several pictures of my family that he had taken from my father's tailor shop after the Germans took us.

Jacob Berger (Solomon's father)

Rosa Fabian Berger (Solomon's mother)

Baby Solomon (center). Brothers Moishe (left) and Joshua (right). Sisters Bella (far left) and Rose (far right). Mother (center) and father (seated). Krosno, Poland, 1921

The Berger Boys. Michael, Solomon, Joshua, and Moishe (left to right)

Berger Family in front of their home. Krosno, Poland. Solomon (top center), Moishe and Rafael (right to left from Solomon), Bella (far left on step), Joshua (bottom left), Rose (bottom center, light coat), father (bottom, top hat), Sonya, Michael, and mother (far right, front to back)

Gideo Soccer Team. Krosno, Poland. Solomon (third from right). Joshua and Michael (far left)

Michael Berger

Solomon and niece Sonya

Solomon (far right) and friends

Solomon Berger

I found the Jewish survivors' apartment in the center of Krosno where I met some young people who all survived the war by hiding in bunkers or attics. "How is life in Poland?" I asked.

"It's tough," a survivor responded. "Anti-Semitism is still the same. Polish people don't want us Jews to come back and demand the return of our properties. The minute the war ends, we will leave Poland toward Jerusalem. In Krakow, a Jewish Committee is assembling survivors and taking them to Romania where ships are waiting."

A man introduced himself as a representative of Bricha, an underground organization that helped survivors escape to Palestine. He kept records and made false papers for anyone that wanted to go. I told him I had been a member of Beitar before the war. He said, "You can be of help. You have open access as a Soviet officer. Our movement is still restricted. Please go to

Warsaw to meet Antek Zuckerman. His Jewish name is Yitzhak, but he is pretending to be a Catholic Polish representative, so his name is Antek. He survived the Warsaw ghetto revolt and is now a member of the Polish Communist Party. Will you see Antek Zuckerman to find out what the Polish Communist Party knows about Zionist movements in Poland?" I said that I would go to Warsaw because I could help. The Bricha representative said that Zuckerman lived at Narsca 38 in the former Warsaw ghetto.

I walked back home to see if my family's house was still standing. At our address, there was just a fenced-in empty lot. The school next door still stood but was closed. I was not angry, only sad. I had grown up in the same house my whole life. Now, just an empty lot.

In Krosno there were no more synagogues, and the only Jewish people were leaving as soon as possible. I thought about where I fit in now. When I was running around trying to survive, I did not ask God to help me. I was lucky. I never made any plans. I managed to go through hell and survive. Religions say that if you help yourself, God will help you too. As a Catholic Pole, I felt more secure than being Jewish. I could remain a Catholic Pole, marry a gentile woman, have Catholic children, live happily ever after. But I thought, "No! No! I can't do that. I can't live a lie all my life. I am not prepared to do that. I was born a Jew and I'm going to die a Jew. When they put me into a casket and cover me with earth, that's the end of it. There is no heaven for me to go to, but I am not scared. If I'm dead, what have I got to be scared of? Believe in God? Maybe I do, maybe I don't. I believe in unknown things. I believe in nature. To me, religion means doing good deeds, being a good person, and helping your fellow man."

Even with my Soviet rifle and handgun, I was afraid to sleep in the Jewish apartment. I spent the night at the Duchowskis'. In the morning, I visited the Bricha representative, who was with a blonde Jewish girl who had survived the German occupation by working in a store and pretending to be Catholic. She made me an official document that said, "Ivan Marianowicz Jerzowski: Member of the Communist Party of Poland." I slept at the Duchowskis' for another night. I said goodbye and hitch-hiked on a military truck going north toward Warsaw. Two days later, I arrived.

The Wisla River divided Warsaw in half. The Soviets were on one side, and Antek's address in the former Warsaw ghetto was on the other. I walked to the river. All the bridges across the Wisla were demolished, so Soviets had put up temporary pon-toon bridges that only military men in uniform could cross. I saw a group of Polish soldiers in four-pointed hats sitting outside a building. As I passed them in my Soviet officer's uniform, I heard a soldier say in Polish amongst themselves, "Jew." After surviving for more than a year without anybody suspecting me, I was shocked that they were able to spot me so easily. I crossed the Wisla River on a platoon bridge into the demolished Warsaw ghetto. I found a half-standing building on Narsca 38.

I met Antek Zuckerman inside. Antek was in his thirties and looked like a good-looking Gestapo man: tall and blond. "I'm Solomon Berger from Krosno," I said. "I'm on leave from the Red Army as Ivan Jerzowski. A Bricha representative from Krosno sent me for information about survivors that are trying to leave Poland." Antek wanted me to find out what the Polish Com-munist Party knew about the Jews' plans to escape to Palestine.

He told me the location of the official Polish government office. I slept in Soviet officers' barracks. The next day, I walked to the address that Antek had provided.

There were guards at the door. I introduced myself as Ivan Jerzowski and showed the guards my Polish Communist Party identification. The guards led me to an office where I met with a Polish government official named Mr. Beirut. "I come from the Red Army," I told him. "My name is Ivan Marianowicz Jerzowski. I am originally from Krosno."

Mr. Beirut interrupted, "From Krosno! You're the man I've been looking for! We know there are representatives of a Zionist movement in Krosno taking Jews out of Poland. We don't want to hurt these Jews, but we need to know who their leaders are."

"I will try to find out," I told him. Antek Zuckerman was the leader of the Zionist movement, but I did not plan to tell Mr. Beirut.

Back at Antek's, we discussed my exchange with Mr. Beirut. Antek asked me to take a group of Jewish survivors on a truck to Lublin and then Krakow. There was a Jewish Committee in Krakow that helped survivors escape Poland. I told Antek I would help. I would leave right away, before new borders were established.

I sat in the passenger seat of a truck traveling southeast with fifteen Jewish survivors, some still wearing striped death camp uniforms. We drove straight through all the Soviet checkpoints without being stopped because I was in my officer's uniform. In Lublin, we picked up fifteen more survivors. Four hours later, we all arrived at the Krakow Jewish Committee. We were taken to safe houses to get some rest. Straw sacks were set up to sleep on. We were given some bread and potatoes to eat. A Bricha representative told us to register at the Committee in the morning to find out if any family members had survived.

CHAPTER TWENTY-FIVE

ברּ

AT FIRST SIGHT

J anuary, 1945, I turned twenty-two. The Red Army came into Katowice and the Germans left. I was still Stanislava Urbanska, a Catholic Pole. "I'm going to look for my family," I told Maria and her family. The only thing that I cared about was finding my family. My plan: go to Tarnopol, find anybody.

There was no transportation, so I hitched a ride with Russian and Polish soldiers. It was nighttime and pouring rain when we arrived in Krakow. A Polish officer said to me, "You can sleep at my house tonight. My wife is there. In the morning, you can see if you can find somebody from your family."

Knowing nobody else in Krakow and not wanting to spend the night in the rain, I accepted the Polish officer's offer. He took me to his house. His wife immediately adopted me like a daughter. I had my own room, clothes to wear, and food to eat. The next day, I discovered a Jewish Committee in town where survivors could register. I made sure nobody followed me. At the Committee building, there was no information about any of my family, but I learned that the

Committee received new information every day. With wonderful accommodations at the Polish officer's house, it was best to remain in Krakow instead of continuing on to Tarnopol.

One night, a Polish professor came to visit the officer's wife. We ate dinner together and continued talking. Then the professor said, "Hitler deserves a statue for all the Jews he killed." I sat frozen as the officer's wife nodded in agreement.

I wanted to yell, "Go to Hell," but instead I said, "Do you know that in prison the Nazis used pliers to pull out the nails of Polish political prisoners? They screamed like you could not imagine. That you didn't see. That you didn't hear."

While at the marketplace buying food for the house, I bumped into Mina's old friend. "Junka," I said, "Don't talk to me here. Where are you staying?" She whispered that she was staying at the Jewish Committee.

I went looking for her the next day. Junka told me she was going to Palestine. I said, "If you ever find my sister, brother, or any of my family, please give them my address." I gave her the Polish officer's address. "Only give my address to my family," I said in a gravely serious tone.

I kept returning to the Jewish Committee, hoping to learn something new about my family.

છે

The next morning, I went to the Krakow Jewish Committee in my Soviet uniform. The Jewish Committee was just a two-room apartment. A man sitting at the front desk looked at my uniform and hesitantly asked in Polish, "Who are you?"

"I want to see a representative," I responded. He took me to the other room to see the woman in charge. Junka sat behind a desk. She appeared to be twenty-five years old, the same age as me. I sat down in front of her desk. Before Junka said anything, I introduced myself. I said, "I am no Russian. My name is Solomon Berger. I am from Krosno. I survived with the partisans for a year and then was inducted into the Red Army." Junka listened and wrote down everything that I said. "I'm on leave right now…"

A beautiful blonde girl walked into the office. She walked over to Junka. They shook hands. They knew each other. The blonde girl was wearing a navy blue dress with white polka dots. She carried herself very innocently. She looked at me with her blue eyes like she was afraid to open her mouth.

෧

A Soviet officer was at the Jewish Committee. Before he said a word, I could tell from his eyes that he thought I was very pretty. He looked only a few years older than me. Junka introduced him as Solomon Berger.

"Will you have lunch with me?" he asked.

"I don't go out with Russians," I quickly responded.

"Junka told you already, I am not a Russian. I am Jewish," he replied.

"I am not having lunch with anybody," I said. I did not want anything to do with him. I did not want him to blow my cover. I turned around, pulled Junka aside to ask about my family, and went back to the Polish officer's house.

ళు

I remained in the office. "Who is that girl?" I asked Junka.

"She is from my hometown of Tarnopol. Her sister was my friend. She is Jewish. Her original name is Gusta Friedman. She survived pretending to be a Catholic girl by the name of Stanislava Urbanska. Everyday, she comes to the Committee to see if her older sister, my friend Mina, may have survived in Germany. Just like you, she also would like to leave Poland, but she's afraid because she doesn't know anybody anywhere or have any money."

"Where does she live?" I asked.

"She lives in Krakow with a Polish woman and her husband who is an officer in the Polish army," Junka responded.

"Tell me her address," I demanded.

"I can't give you the address," Junka said. "I swore to her that I would not tell anybody where she lives…except her family."

"Where does she live?" I continued to demand.

"I cannot tell you! When Gusta told me her address, she made me swear not to tell anyone!" Junka replied.

I did not give up. I continued to ask Junka for Gusta's address. After Junka refused several more times, I insisted. Finally, my persistence paid off because Junka gave me the address. I said goodbye to Junka and left the Krakow Jewish Committee.

I waited at a safe house until nighttime because the curfew was still in effect. The people in Krakow could not walk in the streets after dark. As a Soviet officer, the curfew did not apply to me. I decided to wait until after curfew so Gusta would be at home. After dark, I walked to the address that Junka had given me. It was not far from the Jewish Committee. I decided that I would tell Gusta, "I am going to desert the Red Army and leave Poland. I will take you with me if you want to go."

I knocked on the door.

Someone knocked on the door. I stood in the living room and watched the Polish officer's wife. It was past curfew and we were the only two at home. Solomon Berger was at the door in his Soviet uniform.

"Is Ms. Urbanska here?" he asked.

"We do not have a Ms. Urbanska here," the officer's wife responded. She then tried to close the door. Solomon pushed the door open and walked past the officer's wife toward me. He told the officer's wife to go to her bedroom.

Solomon walked right up to me in the living room and said, "I know who you are. I know that you want to leave Poland, but you don't have any money and are afraid. I also want to leave Poland." He looked directly into my eyes and continued talking, "If you want to leave, I'll take you with me. I will take care of you. Meet me at the Jewish Committee tomorrow morning at ten o'clock." Without waiting for a reply, he walked out just as quickly as he had come in.

After Solomon left, the officer's wife came out of her bedroom. She started to cry on my shoulders. Between her sobs, she said, "I have treated you like my own child. Why did you bring the soviet secret police to my house?" She sobbed, "You will get me in trouble. I can't have you around."

CHAPTER TWENTY-SIX

ↅ

HITLER IS DEAD!

The officer's wife cried all night. As I lay awake in bed, I knew that there was no place for me in her house. I was sorry to go. It was beautiful in Krakow where I could hope everyday to discover news of my family at the Jewish Committee.

The minute it became light outside, I took all my belongings, which was not much, and walked to the Jewish Committee. I sat down beside other survivors and waited.

ↅ

I walked to the Krakow Jewish Committee at ten o'clock the next morning. When I arrived, Gusta was already there. She had a rucksack and looked ready to go. I still hoped that I would be able to marry her. I walked up to Gusta and said, "I'm glad that you're here. I hope that you are coming with me. I'm going to take care of you. Don't worry about anything."

"You did a terrible thing to me," Gusta replied. "I went through hell last night. I had no choice but to come here today."

I took Gusta to the safe house and found her an empty straw sack. We went back to the Jewish Committee and told Junka our plan to leave Poland together. Junka made us both false identification papers that said we were Greek survivors of the concentration camps. It would be easier to book a passage on a boat in Romania as a Greek concentration camp survivor than as a Polish Jew. My new name was Shlomo Harari. Junka said, "'Harari' means Berger in Greek. 'Kalimera' means good morning and 'kalispera' means good afternoon." Even though this was all the Greek we knew, Junka assured us that everybody would be convinced we were Greek.

Gusta and I did not talk much as we walked to the market so that I could buy civilian clothes. I purchased a dark green suit. She continued to be very unhappy that I had forced her out of the Polish officer's house.

We slept in a safe house on separate straw sacks. Fifteen other Jewish survivors shared our room. Many others filled the neighboring rooms in the safe house. Everybody was very skinny. The next day, a Bricha representative led Gusta, me, and a dozen other survivors to the Krakow train station. I did not know any of the others in our group. Half of them still wore their striped concentration camp uniforms. I wore my full Soviet officer uniform. We did not have to purchase train tickets.

A freight train arrived in the station. Every car was packed full of refugees. There was no room to get on. I ordered four Soviet soldiers that were standing around the train station to help me. I selected one of the packed freight cars. With the other soldiers by my side, I held my rifle and ordered everybody out of the car. Fifty people exited the freight car without saying a word. I led my group into the car and closed the door. There was one little barbed window. I knew that freight trains like these had been used to deport my mother, sister, Raphael, and their daughters. The train started traveling southeast towards Czechoslovakia.

℘

Our plan was to travel by train to the Black Sea in Romania where there were boats leaving for Palestine. We wanted to live as Jews without fear. The train continued to travel across a devastated Poland. I did not look out the window. Sitting on the floor of the freight train cattle car, I hoped I would see my family again. I was tired of being a fake person. I knew I was leaving Poland forever.

℘

A few hours later, the train stopped briefly in Krosno. When the train departed the Krosno station, I looked out the little barbed window and said to myself, "This is the last time I will be in Poland. I never want to see this country again."

The train soon crossed the Polish border and traveled south through Czechoslovakia. We did not know what was going to happen. I did not know whether we could accomplish what we were trying to accomplish. I took off my Soviet uniform and put on my new dark green suit. I threw the uniform out of the moving train. I tore up all my documents, except for my Greek identification, and also threw them out the window along with my guns and bottle of vodka. I had started as Solomon Berger, became Jan Jerzowski, and then Ivan Marianowicz Jerzowski. I was now Shlomo Harari, a Greek survivor of the concentration camps.

We stopped for a short time in a Czechoslovakian train station. Many local people had come to the train station to greet the survivors. We remained on board as the locals brought us food, water, and clothes for anyone still in their thin concentration camp clothes.

చ

We departed from our train in a Hungarian town called Debrecen to wait for another train. A Bricha representative placed our group of twenty fake Greek survivors into a school auditorium where the Germans used to keep their horses. There was a lot of straw and horse manure. The first thing we did was clean many of the rooms with whatever we could find. A public kitchen in Debrecen provided us with free food, so we would not starve. There were no beds, or blankets, or furniture of any kind. We slept on the floor.

చ

I walked around Debrecen trying to find out any news about what was happening in Europe. The Hungarians had public transportation and some apartments with toilets and running water. It was more modern than Poland. I heard talk on the streets that Germany was defeated.

Deeply in love with Gusta, I thought about her all the time. At the school auditorium, Gusta and I talked about what was going to happen when we left Debrecen. We talked about getting to the Black Sea in Romania and making it to Palestine. I hoped that she would get to know me better.

May 7, 1945. After a week of sleeping on the floor of the

school auditorium, we awoke to the sound of fireworks. It was close to midnight and we could not leave because of the curfew. At daybreak on May 8, we all walked out of the auditorium to see what was happening. The streets of Debrecen were full of people dancing, hollering, and singing. The Hungarians could only speak Hungarian, so we did not know why the people were celebrating. I spotted some Soviet soldiers and asked them in Russian. The Soviet soldiers said, "The war is over! Germany has capitulated. Hitler is dead!"

PART III:

ๆ

THE AMERICAN DREAM

☙

Chapter Twenty-Seven

OUR WEDDING

We were now free. We no longer had to watch every move we made. We celebrated our new freedom in the streets of Debrecen.

The following day, our group of survivors boarded a regular passenger train toward Romania. Everything was free for concentration camp survivors, so we did not pay for tickets. We traveled southeast four hours until we arrived in the Romanian city of Cluj, the old capital of Transylvania. A Bricha representative led us to a three-story community building in Cluj where we could stay and eat for free. There were fifty other Jews in the community apartment building. Six or seven straw sacks were set up in each room instead of beds. Gusta and I found two sacks in the same room.

Bricha needed one hundred passengers to hire a ship in the city of Constanta on the Black Sea. We had to wait. During the day, I walked around Cluj with Gusta. Cluj was still a beautiful city because the war never hit it. The Romanian fascist regime had joined Hitler's war machine voluntarily, so Germany never attacked or occupied Romania. Our group at the community building waited and planned for our trip to the Black Sea. I took care of Gusta, making sure that nobody attacked or took advantage of her. She continued to be reserved and not very outgoing.

May 17, 1945. A Bricha representative came into the community building and said, "We have bad news. The British Navy has blockaded all ports on the Black Sea. They are not permitting any more Jews to illegally sail toward Palestine. The British are taking ships of survivors to camps. We have to change direction. Now, we have to move you all to Italy where there are more ports. It will be easier to transport you to Palestine from there." Gusta held onto me like I was her savior.

"I am not very pleased with the new arrangements," I said to myself. "I do not want to go to unknown places. Three of my sisters live in Los Angeles. I know I am supposed to go to America." I formulated a new plan. I would continue traveling with the group of survivors because Bricha had already made arrangements, and I did not want to break up the transportation. I would be quiet until I arrived in Italy, then I would prepare immigration applications to the United States.

After we heard the bad news, Gusta prepared sandwiches for a picnic. Gusta and I walked alone to a beautiful park with benches, trees, and a little lake. I lay a blanket down under a tree. As we sat on the blanket under the tree eating sandwiches, I said, "Since we can't go to the Romanian port and now we are going to Italy, I am going to change my plans. Once I get to Italy, I'm going to the United States where I have three sisters living in Los Angeles."

"What do you think I should do?" Gusta asked me.

"You can come with me," I replied. "If you want to go with me, I'll take you. Any place I go, you can go. We can take good care of each other."

"That's fine," she said. "I would like that, I would like to go with you."

I started to get some encouragement. I said, "Before we do anything, I must share something that I have wanted to tell you for the last three weeks, but I've never had enough courage to tell you." I took a big breath and looked into Gusta's beautiful blue eyes.

❧

Solomon looked into my eyes and said, "When I first saw you in Krakow, you looked so beautiful, so innocent. The minute I saw you, I fell in love. Now, since we have been traveling together for the last three weeks, you've gotten to know me better. You see that I'm a decent person. Before we go toward Italy, I want to tell you what I've been wanting to tell you for weeks. I don't know if any of my family survived the war. You don't know if any of your family survived. I need to share my thoughts and feelings with someone. You need to share your thoughts and feelings with someone. It is too painful to be alone. I am in love with you and want to share myself with you. I love you, Gusta Friedman, will you marry me?"

❧

I was not romantic. I was just a twenty-five-year-old grown-up man who had gone through hell for the last five years. I had found a person with whom I could have a beautiful life. Gusta responded to my proposal, "Solomon, you must be out of your mind. I like you too, but you must be crazy! We don't have anything. We don't have a home. We don't have any money. We don't know where we're going to be tomorrow. Why don't we go together until we come to a normal place in life? After we settle, I will marry you. But not now. Now, I don't want to marry you."

ço

"You mean yes?" Solomon said.

"No," I said. "I mean no." All I wanted was to find my family first. I looked at Solomon. I liked him as a friend, but I had never thought of being married to anyone. Furthermore, I was still mad at him for how he had charged into the Polish officer's house in Krakow. He had spoiled everything for me.*

ço

I did not want to lose her. I was afraid that if we waited like she suggested, she would find somebody better than me and it would all be over. I did not want to let her go. I asked her again, "There is nobody left in Poland. If you marry me, we will go to America. We will go to Los Angeles where we will have some family. We can have a good life. Will you marry me?"

ço

Again, I said, "No." But I remained sitting under the tree in the beautiful Romanian town. "Why do you want to marry me?" I asked him.

"When I first saw you at the Krakow Jewish Committee," he said, "you were different from anyone else. My only thought was, 'I am going to marry this girl.' When I asked you out and you refused me, something told me that I could not just let you go."

I said, "I still want to wait to get married."

⁘

I told Gusta, "I am a very capable person. When we get to America, I will make a good living. We will raise a family. We will start living a normal and beautiful life. I would like to marry you now." After Gusta again said that she wanted to wait, I would not let it go. I was very persistent.

⁘

I kept refusing his proposals, but we remained sitting under the tree. I looked at him. I looked him all over. I listened to him ask me to marry him again. I refused him again, but I did not walk away. As I sat under the tree, listening to Solomon ask me to marry him over and over, I wondered why I did not leave. I had nowhere to go. He was guiding me. He again asked me to marry him, and I refused again. But we remained sitting under the tree. I looked at him and listened to another of his attempted proposals. As he was speaking, I knew without any doubt that he was an honest person. After too many refusals to count, I finally said, "Yes... I will marry you."

⁘

We both stood up and hugged each other. Then, we kissed for the first time.

❧

Was I in love? I don't know. I was young and alone. Maybe God was telling me to stay under the tree. Maybe I did not know what else to do, except finally say yes. The only thing I knew was that I trusted him to take care of me.

❧

We decided that we would get married right away because if one of us was in trouble, we could defend each other as husband and wife. Also, we knew that married couples always got their own space, while single people shared rooms. We packed up our blanket and walked back to the community building. When we arrived, we looked for somebody to marry us. I saw a survivor in his mid-thirties who looked like a rabbi. I asked him, "Are you a rabbi?"

"Yes, I'm a rabbi," he said.

"Can you marry somebody?" I responded.

"Anytime you want to marry somebody, I can marry somebody," the rabbi told me. "Now, do you have a ring?"

"I don't have a ring," I said.

"How are you going to marry somebody if you don't have a ring?" the rabbi asked me.

I started to ask all the other survivors at the community building, "Does anyone have a ring?" I soon found someone with a plain gold ring who said that I could borrow it. Gusta and I found two from our group who agreed to be witnesses. The two witnesses, rabbi, Gusta, and I then walked to the same tree in the park where I had proposed.

Gusta and I stood with the rabbi under the tree. The rabbi said a Hebrew prayer and then told me to place the ring on Gusta's finger. As I placed the gold band on Gusta's ring finger, I repeated after the rabbi as he said in Hebrew, "Behold, you are consecrated to me with this ring according to the laws of Moses and Israel." The rabbi then said to us, "You are married. Kiss the bride."

Gusta and I kissed for the second time ever.

ITALY

The day after our wedding, a Bricha representative led all the survivors from the community building to the Cluj train station. We boarded a passenger train and traveled southwest to Belgrade, Yugoslavia. The bridge across the Danube in Belgrade was dismantled, so we could not go farther. The original plan was to take an hour plane ride from Belgrade to southern Italy, but after arriving in Belgrade, we learned that the British had discontinued flights. We had to travel by train. Our group was placed in a Belgrade Jewish community center where food and money were provided.

Gusta and I walked to a marketplace and bought some fruit. Belgrade had returned to normal life. Tito's partisans fought the Germans during the whole war and had now taken over the rule of the town. After a week in Belgrade, our group took a train northwest for half a day to Zagreb. We changed trains and soon crossed the Yugoslavian border into Italy. We stopped in a small northern Italian town called Udine.

At the Udine station, the Jewish Brigade of the British Army registered all the survivors, gave us food, and provided clothes for anybody who needed them. The Jewish Brigade put us on trucks to Bologna and then a train to Bari in southern Italy. From Bari, we were driven to a displaced persons camp, Santa Maria di Bagni, in a southeastern Italian fishing village on the edge of the Adriatic Sea.

Fifteen hundred other Jewish refugees lived in Santa Maria di Bagni. The camp consisted of many villas that had been used as an Italian fascist resort. Gusta and I were placed in a crowded community building that we named La Chofesh because "Chofesh" means freedom in Hebrew. Everyone at the camp planned on going to Palestine, but Gusta and I secretly planed on immigrating to the United States.

There was one beautiful villa close by where all married couples were getting their own rooms. Within the first few days at the camp, Gusta and I managed to get a private room in the nearby villa and were given access to food provisions from a warehouse. We then registered in the camp office for immigration to the United States. The United Nations Relief and Rehabilitation Administration provided free breakfast to all the refugees staying at the camp, but Gusta usually prepared a private breakfast in our room. After breakfast, many survivors went down to the beach to forget the terrible horrors that they had just experienced.

Gusta (right) and friend in Italy

Solomon (standing, third to right) with his Italian soccer team

Pro Israel demonstration at Santa Maria di Bagni

Solomon (middle) on the Adriatic Sea

Instead of spending my days at the beach, I got a job at the canteen near the shore. I sold foods, like fruit or chocolate, to refugees who wanted an extra snack. The American Joint Distribution Committee paid me only ten dollars a month, but we did not have to pay for lodging or food, so any money I made was extra pocket money.

One day at work, I could see a large bunch of Jewish refugees from the camp surrounding a man at the beach. The group began savagely beating him. I left the canteen to find out what was going on. Keeping my distance, I learned that the guy getting beaten up had been swimming in the sea without a top. When he lifted his arms in the water, some refugees saw an SS tattoo under his armpit. The Italian SS had been trying to hide among Jewish survivors. The refugees had pulled him out of the water. I watched as they beat him to death. They then left him alone on the beach. When the police showed up, everyone had already dispersed and nobody would tell the Italian authorities what happened. I thought the SS man should have been arrested to face justice instead of getting killed, but I did not want to get involved.

A few months later, representatives from a Jewish left-wing group called Haganah entered the camp and started to register the survivors. They wanted to know what organizations we had belonged to before the war. I registered as a former member of Beitar. Although Gusta and I wanted to go to the United States, we would have happily gone to Palestine first.

After another couple months, the Haganah representatives came back to put refugees onto little boats which transported them to larger boats in the Adriatic Sea. Haganah was trying to illegally smuggle the Jewish refugees into Palestine. Gusta and I

were not selected because I was ineligible as a former member of
the right-wing Beitar. As it turned out, the British Navy stopped
or drowned most of the Haganah ships and took the Jewish refugees on board to Cyprus where they were treated like criminals.
Fortunately, Gusta and I remained safe in Santa Maria di Bagni,
waiting for our opportunity to go to America.

Spring, 1946. I found out that Gusta was pregnant. She was
scared and worried about how we were going to raise a child. I
knew that everything was going to work out all right.

August 24, 1946. Gusta gave birth to a boy. We named him
Jacob in memory of my father. We called him Jackie. He was born
in an Italian hospital run by survivor doctors and nun nurses.

While Gusta and Jackie were still in the hospital, I wanted to
make Gusta a soup. I got a chicken, cut off its head, took all the
feathers off, cut it apart, and starting cooking it in an old kettle.
I did not know how to cook. I kept putting in more and more
salt. I took the chicken soup to the hospital and gave it to Gusta.

࿐

When I was still in the hospital after giving birth, Solomon
brought me a chicken soup that he had made himself. He watched
me through the window to see if I would eat it. I tried the soup. It
was so salty that I thought he had boiled seawater and served it to me.
I poured the soup out when he was not looking.

࿐

After Gusta and Jackie came home from the hospital, I traveled to a nearby town to buy baby clothes. At a flea market, I

purchased a beautiful baby outfit and put it down to pick out something else. When I turned around, somebody had stolen the outfit. I did not have much money left, so I bought what baby clothes I could afford. I brought back the clothes to Gusta who said, "That's what you think Jackie's worth!? How could you bring such stupid clothes back here?"

"I'm sorry," I said. "I bought a beautiful outfit, but someone stole it from me. I didn't have enough money to buy anything else." Gusta accepted my response.

℘

Gusta, Solomon, and baby Jackie

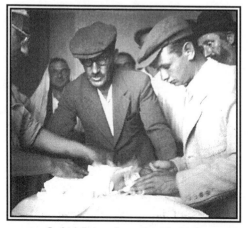

Jackie's Briss. September 10, 1946

Gusta and Jackie, Santa Maria di Bagni, Italy

The soldiers' barracks were long buildings that were hot both day and night. At night, when one person turned on a lamp, everyone could see the light. We did not have a stove, so I built fires. Anytime I wanted to cook, I placed two bricks on the fire and cooked with Crisco cans and jars instead of pots and pans. I also boiled water in Crisco cans to wash Jackie's diapers by hand.

&

After a year and a half in Santa Maria di Bagni, the Italian government liquidated the camp and moved all refugees to barracks in a transit camp closer to Bari. Every barrack was split into twelve rooms with walls that only went halfway to the ceiling. Single people were two or three to a room. Married couples got our own rooms, but everyone could hear each other.

I obtained a new job as a men's clothing and design instructor for ORT, a Jewish organization that provided vocational training in displaced persons camps. Two days a week, I taught a class at the transit camp. Two other days a week, I taught at another displaced persons camp near Barletta. To get to Barletta, I rode a bicycle to the Bari train station and then took a train an hour northwest. I had learned enough broken Italian to make myself understood. The Italians kept telling me, "You speak Italian molto bene," and always treated me wonderfully. At the Barletta train station, I left my bicycle near the station and walked to the barracks to teach. My students were all Jewish survivors. The American Joint Distribution Committee paid me thirty dollars a month to teach the ORT tailoring classes.

One day a Jewish Palestinian soldier from Krosno came into

the transit camp to see if he knew any of the refugees. We recognized each other. He told me that, in 1938, he had immigrated to Palestine. When the war broke out in 1939, he had volunteered for the Jewish Brigade of the British Army and was currently stationed near Bari, but would be discharged soon. Gusta told him that she had an aunt and cousins in Palestine. The soldier said, "In Palestine, there are radio announcements everyday. An announcer reads the names of Jewish survivors who are looking for their families."

ↁↄ

Solomon wrote a note for the Palestinian soldier that said, "Gusta Friedman, married now to Solomon Berger. Survived. From Tarnopol. She is living in a displaced persons camp near Bari, Italy. She is with a child." The soldier took the note and returned to Palestine.

Everyday, I prayed that I would find Mina or anyone from my family. I prayed that if something happened to me, my baby would know my family.

A sister of my father lived in Palestine and happened to be listening to the radio when she heard the announcement with my name. My aunt immediately got in touch with her sister in England, my Auntie Tony, who had moved to London from Vienna in 1938 right after Hitler took over. Auntie Tony contacted me in Italy. She told me that my sister, Mina, was alive.

ↁↄ

November, 1946. I finally made contact with my sister Frances in Los Angeles through the Red Cross. I sent Frances a letter saying that I had survived, was married with a child in a DP camp in Italy, and would like to go to the United States as quickly as possible. Soon after, I received an affidavit of support from Frances. A Red Cross representative advised me to take the affidavit of support to the American Consulate in Naples to get United States visas. Gusta, little baby Jackie, and I traveled right away to Naples, where we registered for immigration to the United States using our original names.

The American consulate was very friendly when he told us, "I'm not permitted to issue any visas yet. We have to take all soldiers and military equipment back home from war first. I will place you on a waiting list. Go back to the camp and wait until we notify you. Then, you'll be able to come pick up your visas and immigrate to the United States." We had no choice but to go back to the barracks. I was frustrated that we could not go straight to America.

A Red Cross representative also notified me that my brother Michael had survived. Michael had survived the concentration camps and now lived in Los Angeles working as a tailor. I felt that Michael was luckier than me, because he was already in Los Angeles. Michael and I began writing letters back and forth in Polish. He wrote that when I came to America, he would get me a job. We could not wait to be reunited. My sisters Eleanor and Frances also sent me letters. I could not speak English, so we communicated in German. Every month they each sent me a letter with a two-dollar bill. Gusta and I never spent any money, so we were able to save almost all my ORT salary and the two-dollar bills we received from my sisters.

While I went to work, Gusta stayed home taking care of

our baby. Jackie was a terrible eater and Gusta was always worrying. Gusta would bring Jackie to the soccer field near the barracks where I played right defense, leave Jackie with me, and say, "You play with him!" Little Jackie and I had a lot of fun playing soccer together.

We lived in the barracks for the next year and a half. During this time, I became friends with a young Jewish welfare officer from London who was in charge of all ORT instructors.

Early summer, 1947. The welfare officer said to me, "Berger, if you want to go to London, I have a brother-in-law there who is quite wealthy. I can make arrangements for you to go work for him in London."

"It's about time," I responded. "I have been in Italy for three years now. I will go anywhere to get out of here." The welfare officer took all my details. A short time later, I received a request from the officer's brother-in-law in London, Mr. Myman, to hire Gusta and me as a domestic resident couple. I would be a butler and Gusta would be a maid. I did not want to be a butler, but we were happy to finally leave the Italian camps.

Gusta, Jackie, and I went to the English consulate in Rome. We were told that we needed proper Polish passports to get English visas. We then went to the Polish consulate in Rome, where they sent a request to Poland for a copy of our birth certificates. I received my birth certificate from Krosno, but Gusta's could not be located. Fortunately, the consulate issued us both passports. Even though they wrote that Gusta's name was Guta, we were happy to have finally obtained our Polish passports and immigration papers for England. We used the two-dollar bills we had accumulated to purchase train tickets and some nice things to help us settle in London.

2

Rysopis — Signalements

Data urodzenia
Date de naissance | *28.X. 1919*

Miejsce urodzenia
Lieu de naissance | *KROSNO*

Stan
Etat civil | *żonaty — marié*

Zatrudnienie
Profession | *instruktor kroju krawieckiego — instructeur de coupure*

Wzrost
Taille | *średni — moyenne*

Twarz
Visage | *owalna — ovale*

Włosy
Cheveux | *szatyn — chatain*

Oczy
Yeux | *piwne — bruns*

Znaki szczególne
Signes particuliers | */.*

Dzieci — Enfants

Imię	Wiek	Płeć
Nom	Age	Sexe
/.	/.	/.

Solomon's Polish Passport, description page

Solomon's Passport Photograph

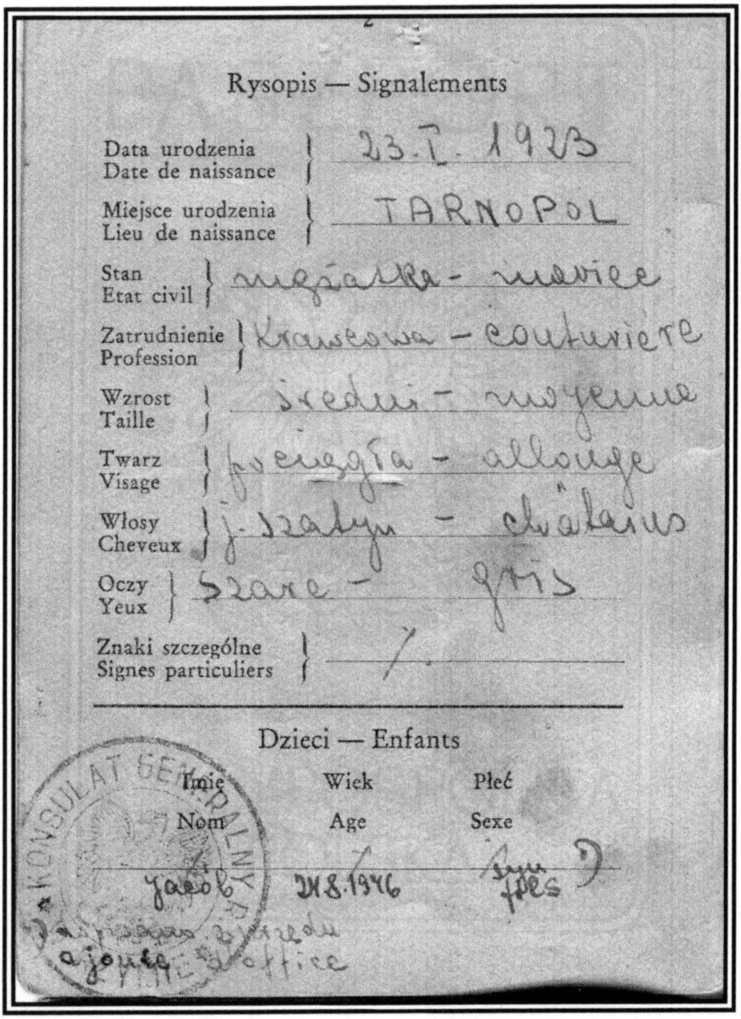

Rysopis — Signalements

Data urodzenia / Date de naissance	23.I.1923
Miejsce urodzenia / Lieu de naissance	TARNOPOL
Stan / Etat civil	mężatka - mariée
Zatrudnienie / Profession	krawcowa - couturière
Wzrost / Taille	średni - moyenne
Twarz / Visage	pociągła - allongée
Włosy / Cheveux	j. szatyn - châtains
Oczy / Yeux	szare - gris
Znaki szczególne / Signes particuliers	./.

Dzieci — Enfants

Imię / Nom	Wiek / Age	Płeć / Sexe
Jacob	21.8.1946	męs. / fils

KONSULAT GENERALNY

Gusta and Jackie's Polish Passport, description page

Gusta's Passport Photo

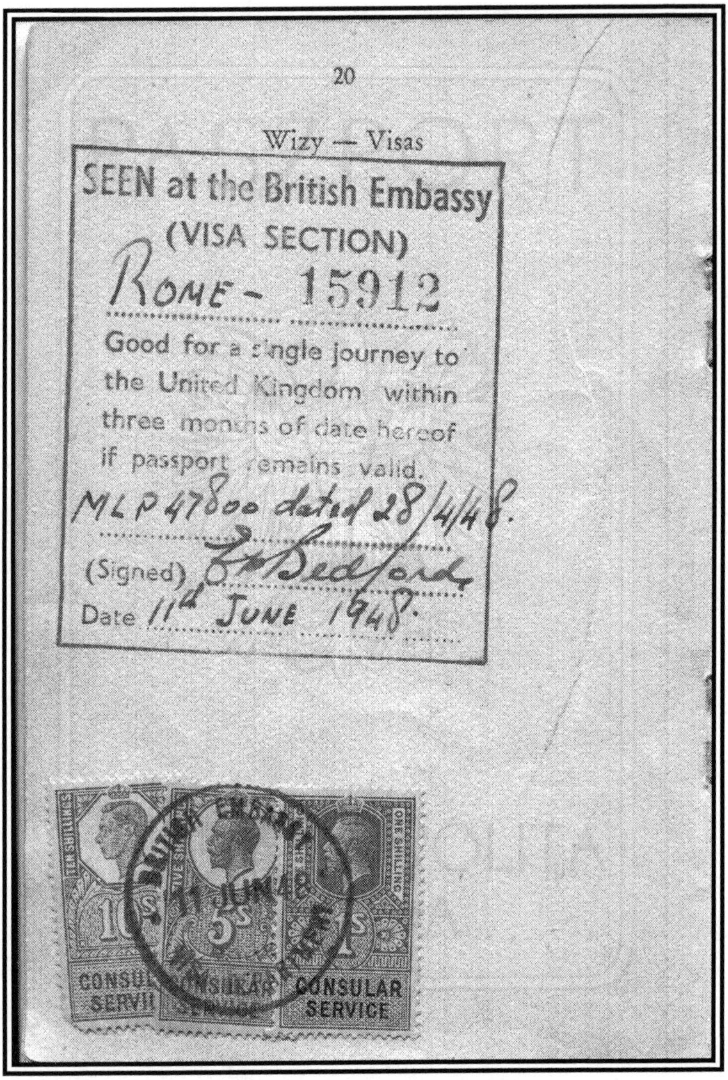

UK Visa (from the British Embassy in Rome)

CHAPTER TWENTY-NINE

卍

LONDON

We took a train from Bari through Geneva and Paris to Calais by the English Channel. The train arrived late at Calais. The passengers rushed to get on the boat going across the Channel. We did not know where the French porter had put our luggage, so Gusta would not let him off the boat until he returned it. The boat left and took the porter all the way to England.

August 23, 1948. Gusta, Jackie, and I arrived in Dover with all our luggage. We took a train right from the boat all the way to Victoria Station in central London. Auntie Tony and Uncle Leo met us at Victoria Station and took us to their small two-bedroom apartment. If we wanted to use gas, electricity, or water, we had to use tokens. The next day, I got in touch with Mr. Myman, our employer, to inform him that we had arrived. He invited us to his house in Stratford, on the far outskirts of London, to have lunch with him and his wife.

UK Entry Visa, Dover, England

Our first weekend in England, we traveled to Mr. Myman's house in Stratford with Auntie Tony. Mr. Myman was a kind and wealthy man in his forties. After lunch, Mr. Myman's wife handed me an envelope. I did not open the envelope until we were back at Auntie Tony's apartment. There were twenty-five English pounds inside, a lot of money at the time, and a beautiful note wishing Gusta, Jackie, and me a lot of happiness in the new country.

On Monday morning, I went with Mr. Myman to his be-spoke tailor, Mr. Pinken, who had a shop on Jermyn Street near Piccadilly Circus. Mr. Pinken was a short English Jew in his late forties. Mr. Myman said to Mr. Pinken, "I brought a couple here from Italy as domestics, but I don't need them. Mr. Berger is a brilliant tailor. I would like you to hire him here in your shop." Mr. Pinken agreed.

Mr. Myman and I then went to the labor department office in London. Mr. Myman told an officer, "I brought a couple here from Italy to work as a domestic couple, but it took so long for them to arrive that I hired somebody else. I would like permis-sion for the couple to change employers from me to Mr. Pinken." The officer approved the change. Mr. Myman and I returned to the tailor shop. Mr. Pinken would pay me fifteen pounds per week in cash because I was registered as a domestic, not a tailor.

I began working immediately at Mr. Pinken's shop with his ten other employees. Mr. Pinken's fashionable clientele picked out materials, got measured in the fitting room, and then we made their custom suits to measure. I happily worked at the bespoke tailor shop six days a week, Sunday through Friday. Each morn-ing, Gusta prepared me a sandwich for lunch before I boarded a double-decker bus. The bus only cost two and a half pence each way. If there were no available seats on a bus, I had to wait for the next one. England was well organized and the British people were very polite. Nobody cut in front of anyone else in line.

There were plenty of buses in London, so I never had to wait long. While I was working, Gusta took Jackie to parks or his nursery school where she worked part-time to pay for his lessons.

Auntie Tony and Uncle Leo's flat was too small for all of us, so Auntie Tony looked every day for an apartment for Gusta, Jackie, and me. I expected her to find one easily because there were plenty of "to let" signs around. However, when I came home from work each night, Auntie Tony said, "I'm sorry. I couldn't get you an apartment today." After three weeks, I suspected that something must be wrong.

"On Saturday," I said to Auntie Tony, "I am going with you to see why we can't rent an apartment." The next Saturday, Auntie Tony and I walked to a nearby apartment with a "to let" sign.

Auntie Tony said to the landlord, "My relatives have come from the continent. They survived the concentration camps. They're such nice people." The landlord immediately responded that the apartment had just been rented. I understood why it had been so hard for Auntie Tony to find us an apartment, she kept telling landlords that we had come directly from the camps.

"Auntie Tony, no more," I told her as we left. "I will go find an apartment myself." The next Saturday, I walked into the first apartment I saw with a "to let" sign. It was completely furnished and available for thirty shillings a week. I told the landlord that I made fifteen pounds a week. I got the apartment.

Gusta, Jackie, and I moved into the new flat and started to live almost a normal life in England. There was still food rationing left over from the war. Our family received two eggs a week because we had a child. There was no steak, but we could get as many rabbits as we wanted. We ate a lot of rabbits. They tasted just like chicken. I continued to work six days a week, while Gusta and Jackie went to the nursery school. On Saturdays in summer, Gusta made sandwiches and we took the number five bus from in front of our apartment to a park where we had picnics or went swimming.

જી

Life in England was horrible. The worst part was the weather and the dirty air. Whenever I hung up our clothes outside to dry, I came back to find them covered in soot. I had to wash and scrub the clothes a second time. Our whole building only had one bath on the second floor. To help us save money, I made soup with leftovers. The best part about living in London was seeing my Auntie Tony. It was so wonderful to be around my family again.

We had been living in England for five months, when a policeman knocked on the door in the middle of the afternoon on a weekday. The policeman said, "Please tell your husband to come to the police station with all your documents."

"He is at work," I responded.

"That's okay," the policeman said. "He can come anytime on Saturday when he is not working. Make sure you tell him to bring all your documents." The policeman left. I was scared that we would be kicked out of our new apartment.

જી

Gusta told me that I had to go to the police station on Saturday with all our documents. I told her that there was nothing to worry about. All refugee survivors had to obtain visa extensions every six months. The next Saturday, I went to the police station. A policeman said to me, "You are here on a permit as a domestic resident couple. You should be living at the address of your employment. However, you are not living at Mr. Pinken's residence?"

"I go to work everyday," I quickly responded, "but Mr. Pinken doesn't have a big enough house. He permits us to stay outside of his house as long as I work everyday."

"I know you go to work everyday, Mr. Berger," the policeman responded. He asked more questions that I answered in half-English. It was easier for me to understand English than to speak it, but I knew enough to communicate. After a half an hour interview, the policeman said, "Please, wait here. I'll come back." Fifteen minutes later, he came back and returned our passports with a stamped permit that entitled Gusta, Jackie, and me to permanent residence in the United Kingdom. I could not believe that we had managed to get permanent residence. We could become British citizens.

Jackie (front, far left) with classmates in English school

UK Permanent Residence & Embarked Stamp

After living in London for a year, I started to earn extra money doing private tailoring work for another refugee that I had met in Italy. He was a master tailor. He had a sewing machine in his house and private customers. I was doing very well in London. In the summer of 1949, I took a one-week vacation. Gusta, Jackie, and I visited the Tower of London and Hyde Park where music played on speakers all day long.

                                                           ভ

October, 1949. Auntie Tony, Uncle Leo, Jackie, and I flew to Frankfurt to see Mina. I was so excited to see my sister again. I had not seen her since she snuck away from the work camp in Tarnopol a few days before me. Mina was married to her second husband, Paul Rotenberg, and was pregnant with a baby girl. She had not seen her first husband since he ran away to fight the Germans. She had divorced him after the war before remarrying.

It was beyond good to see Mina and to hear her voice again. I knew that if anything happened to me, Jackie would now have someone from my family to help look after him. My prayers had been answered.

Mina told us that after she escaped the work camp, she boarded a freight train going to Germany. She traveled without any documents or belongings. When she arrived at the German border, she was allowed to cross. The Gestapo were kind to her, unlike to me. Mina arrived in Germany and was assigned to work on a farm for a German Nazi. She changed her name and worked as a Russian farm girl until the end of the war.

I do not know how she was able to fool everyone into thinking she was Russian. In school, we had learned Ukrainian, not proper Russian. I do not know how she managed to fit in with the other Russian women on the farm. She was so delicate. If she went to milk a cow, and the cow kicked and spilled all the milk, how would she have known what to do? Fortunately, the Russian girls were smart. They helped her survive. When Mina was on the train, the Russian girls took off the buttons from her shirt because the Germans were sending women with buttons back to Russia. I imagined her Nazi boss after the war when he found out that she was Jewish. If only I could have seen his face.

After the war, Mina ran into an English soldier and happened to say hello to him in Hebrew. The soldier answered back in Hebrew. She told him that she had survived the war and had an aunt in England but did not know her address. She gave the soldier Auntie Tony's name. The soldier wrote to his wife in England and she found Auntie Tony in London.

In December, Jackie, Auntie Tony, and I had to go back to England. I did not want to leave my sister now that I had found her, but I knew that I would see her again.

VISITOR NO FACILITIES
VISITEUR SANS PRESTATIONS
BESUCHER KEINE VERGUNSTIGUNGEN
Compassionate visit, no facilities.

Wizy — Visas

GUTA   BERGER
JACOB BERGER (SON)

No. E. 20371

Permit to enter the US, British, French Zone (s)
of Germany.
Permis d'entrée en zone (s) Americaine,
Britanniques, Francaise d'Allemagne.
Einreiseerlaubnis für die Amerikanische,
Britische, Französische Zone (n) Deutschlands.

Valid for one return journey
Valable pour un voyage aller et retour
Gültig für eine Hin- und Rückreise

before
avant le
vor dem

12. Nov. 49

Destination
Bestimmungsort

US. ZONE

Date   12 Oct. 49

Allied ... Commission
PERMIT OFFICE

Military Permit Office   25
LONDON

18 OCT. 1949
389
GERMANY (B.Z.)

Gusta and Jackie's German Visa

Jackie in Frankfurt with family friend

Mina, Gusta, Paul (Mina's husband), Jackie, Auntie Tony, and Uncle Leo (left to right). Frankfurt, Germany

ↁ

When Gusta and Jackie came back from their trip to visit Mina, Jackie was already speaking German. He told us that he only wanted to travel by taxi.

In May of 1950, we received a notice from the American Consulate in London advising us that they were prepared to issue us immigration visas to the United States. We had been on the waiting list since registering in Naples three and a half years before. We presented ourselves at the American Consulate. After an interview, the Consulate finally issued us visas to immigrate to the United States.

Gusta and I liquidated all our belongings to prepare for immigration. I had an expensive Philips radio and kept writing letters to Michael asking him whether America had AC or DC. Michael told me that my radio was not going to work in America, because they used 110 volts and England used 220. I sold my radio and all my other electronic equipment.

As we prepared to leave, I met with Mr. Myman. We had kept in touch the whole time I was in England. I said to him, "I came to say goodbye. We are finally going to go to America."

"Berger," Mr. Myman said, "you are mad to leave London. I've gotten to know you. You are a very capable man, especially in comparison to the British people. All they want is to get out of work, get their fish and chips, and go to the races or football matches on Saturday. They are always waiting for the next weekend to do it all over again. Take me as an example. I immigrated to London in 1938 from Vienna. Since then, I have become a rich manufacturer of plastics. My company is traded on the stock market in England. If you remain here in London, you'll become very rich, just like me. In America, you will be just like all the other hard workers there. You will struggle to make a living. I advise you to stay in England."

"Mr. Myman," I replied. "I would love to stay in England, but I don't have anybody here. The only survivors of my family are my three sisters and my brother in America. I feel that is where I should go. I'm going to make a living in the United States just like I did here."

Mr. Myman said goodbye and wished me the best of luck. I used most of my money to book passages on an ocean liner called the Nieuw Amsterdam that traveled from Southampton all the way to New York.

CHAPTER THIRTY

✌

COMING TO AMERICA

*W*e *bought tickets as normal immigrant passengers and not as refugees. In May 1950, we boarded the Nieuw Amsterdam and left London for the United States.*

✌

The Nieuw Amsterdam was a huge thirty-five-thousand-ton cruise ship with two different passenger classes: tourist or first. We booked the tourist class. We had our own room with no windows. We needed to save our money to start a new life in Los Angeles.

It would take seven days to cross the Atlantic. While we traveled west, Gusta and I dropped Jackie off every morning at a nursery in the first-class area and picked him up in the evening. Gusta went back to our room and threw up all day from seasickness. I felt fine, but there was not much to do. I watched the water speed by as I thought about finally going to America and reuniting with my family. In the evening, we all went to dinner together. I ordered a steak for the first time in my life. The steak was like a stone, so hard I could hardly chew it. The rest of the food on the ship was no better.

Half a day before our scheduled arrival, I stood on deck watching America approach on the horizon. I was filled with positive hope as the ship sailed past the Statute of Liberty and into a free country. "I'm one hundred percent sure I'm going to succeed in this beautiful country," I said to myself. "I'm going to meet my family and start a new life."

જ

June 17, 1950. We arrived in Hoboken, New Jersey. American Immigration officers boarded the ship. Representatives of the Hebrew Immigration Aid Society, HIAS, also boarded. When it was our turn to talk to the officers, we handed them our Polish passports. An officer said to a HIAS representative, "HIAS! Here are your Bergers. You can take them out. Their uncle is waiting outside for them." The American Immigration officer then stamped our passports and we walked with the HIAS representative off the Nieuw Amsterdam.

Solomon's young cousin and old uncle stood waiting for us on the other side of a fence. Solomon's uncle was a tall man with a long white beard that went all the way down to his chest. Jackie looked at his beard and asked, "Daddy, is this Santa Claus?"

જ

My uncle was married to my father's sister. He took us back to his apartment in Brooklyn. My aunt and uncle, both almost ninety years old, were very religious people. My uncle took me right away to his temple to thank God for surviving the terrible war. "I had a son that got killed. He was in the air force," my uncle told me. "Now, I'm gaining another son."

U.S. Immigration Visa and Admitted Stamp

Gusta, Jackie, and I spent a week in Brooklyn with my uncle and aunt, their six children, and many grandchildren. Their name was Horkheiser. I made contact with one of my mother's sisters, Yetta Buckfeld, who lived in the Bronx. We stayed in the Bronx with Yetta for a week. We took a train from New York to Chicago, where four of my mother's brothers lived.

Several of my cousins picked us up at the Chicago train station and took us home. During the next week, we visited with my uncles' large family full of children and grandchildren. I purchased train tickets on the El Capitan that would take us to Los Angeles. All my family came to the Chicago station to see us off.

∾

At the train station in Chicago, everybody gave us envelopes for good luck. On the train we opened them to find coins. One relative gave us fifty cents and another gave us a dollar. One relative gave us two dollars. All together, the envelopes contained thirty dollars. This was all the money we had after buying the train tickets.

∾

I was bored as we traveled west across America. The El Capitan had no sleeping accommodations. For most of the journey, we just sat in our uncomfortable seats. We sometimes walked to a restaurant in a different car. Forty hours later, on a Tuesday in June, 1950, the El Capitan finally arrived at Union Station in downtown Los Angeles.

At the station stood my sister Frances, her husband, Willy, my brother Michael, and his wife, Mildred. When we exited the train, the sun was shining. I could see beautiful trees everywhere. We had finally arrived in a new world. Michael and I hugged each other like two men do. As we walked together to the parking lot, Michael pulled me aside and said, "Don't tell anyone how you survived or what it was like during the war."

"Why?" I asked.

"When I came to America," Michael responded, "I told everybody about how bad it was in Europe and about how I starved. They told me, 'We had a tough time here in America too. We had rations for steak and gasoline, so don't complain that you didn't eat very much.' You will hear the same thing."

∫

Frances and Willy had parked their brand new Oldsmobile next to Michael's beat up Pontiac. Jackie said, "Look at these two cars!" Jackie turned to Michael, pointed at the old Pontiac, and said, "Is this your car? My Daddy is going to have a nicer car than you!" Jackie then pointed at Frances and Willy's Oldsmobile and said, "We're going to have a car like this one."

Frances looked at Jackie and said, "You should go sell papers. Or you could mow lawns."

"If I make money, I make big money," little four-year-old Jackie replied. We all got into Frances and Willy's car and drove to their house where we would stay.

∫

That night, my sister Eleanor organized a dinner for the whole family. I was reunited with my three surviving sisters, Eleanor,

Frances, and Rose, and my one surviving brother, Michael, and all their families. I had been without any relations for so long. Gusta was afraid as she was thrown into a new family, country, language, and life. I kept telling her, "You are my wife and Jackie is my son. I will always take good care of both of you."

The next morning, my brother-in-law, Willy, said to me, "We are going on a trip across the country in our new car for the next two months. We want you to stay in our house. Now, Solomon, we are going to get you a job." Willy then took me to a custom Italian tailor shop on Olympic Boulevard near Western Avenue. It was a fancy shop that specialized in Italian tailoring. Willy said to the Italian owner, "My brother-in-law just came from London. He's an excellent tailor and I want you to give him a job."

"Can he do repairs?" the owner asked.

"He can do anything," Willy responded.

The owner gave me a job for one dollar an hour. I worked at the tailor shop for two weeks before getting fired because I could not tailor to the fancy Italian standards of the owner. The next morning, Michael took me to a women's clothing factory in downtown Los Angeles where he worked. He told his boss that I was a good tailor and asked his boss to hire me. After a long fight to get the union's permission, the boss gave me a job as a sewing machine operator.

I had no idea how to handle the high-power sewing machines in the factory or make women's clothes. All the other workers, including Michael, produced ten to twelve full ladies coats per day. The first day, I could not even make one. I constantly broke needles on the power machines. My boss stood on the side watching me and probably thinking, "Who the hell did I take on here? He knows nothing!" But my boss gave me a chance. I soon learned how to handle the machines and became one of the best workers in the factory. The job paid $7,500 a year, which I thought was a lot of money.

Gusta and I immediately began looking for an apartment of our own. Nobody wanted to rent to people with children. It was also hard to find an apartment because we were Jewish. One day, I was looking at an apartment in a big building on Rodeo, near La Cienega, with a "For Rent" sign. In the leasing office, I saw another sign that read, "Jews do not need to apply." I felt terrible that anti-Semitism was happening all over the world. At least in America, Jews could fight back. A country club on Beverly Boulevard would not admit Jewish people, so the Jews of Los Angeles opened their own country club at Hillcrest and told them to keep their country club to themselves. Fortunately, Gusta and I were able to finally find an apartment that would accept us prior to Frances and Willy's return from their cross-country road trip.

Early in 1951, I found out that Gusta was pregnant again. On a Saturday morning in July, I went to an oral surgeon for a tooth infection. I did not expect Gusta to have the baby for another two or three weeks. After the surgeon pulled out one of my teeth, my mouth was swollen up like a balloon. While I lay in bed on pain medication, Gusta started to have birth pains. I could not get up or drive, so I called Michael. He took Gusta to Cedars-Sinai Hospital.

9:00 pm, July 21, 1951. I received a call from the hospital. A doctor said, "You just had a baby girl!"

"Thank you," I said and fell back to sleep. A few days later, Gusta came home with our daughter. I hired a nurse to stay with

Gusta for a month because I had to go to work and did not want Gusta to be alone.

ఆ

We named her Marlene Rose in honor of my mother and Solomon's mother. We chose Marlene instead of Miriam because there were already too many Miriams in Los Angeles named after a different grandmother.

ఆ

Gusta and I were able to save enough money from my factory job to purchase a two-bedroom condominium on Sherbourne Drive for only $8,000, with an $1,800 down payment. I also bought a used car for $200. In the summertime, between clothing seasons, I got extra work making pattern samples for the factory. I was one of their best workers.

Every summer, Gusta, Jackie, Marlene, and I vacationed in Crestline near Lake Arrowhead. Sometimes we took Michael's sons, Ron and Jeffrey. One summer while swimming in the beautiful lake, I saw a big housing development on the opposite shore. Large signs read, "Reservations Accepted for Purchase." I drove to the other side of the lake and went into the sales office to ask for information about purchasing one of the homes. A salesman told me the total costs for the down payment and mortgage. He asked my name for the official offer.

"Solomon Berger," I said.

"Oh, wait a second," he responded, "I have to call the manager." The salesman and his manager briefly talked in private.

The manager walked over to me and said, "I'm sorry. All the houses are sold out." There was nothing I could say to the obvious anti-Semitism. I walked out and drove back to the other side of the lake.

Jackie and sister Marlene. Los Angeles, California

CHAPTER THIRTY-ONE

ల

AUSCHWITZ

"You know, that letter you sent to me in the SS training camp almost got me killed," Michael said to me one day as we worked next to each other at the factory.

"What happened?" I asked. "How did you get out alive?"

While we continued to sew women's coats, Michael responded, "The Gestapo intercepted the letter and started to beat me up in the training camp. They kept asking, 'Where is your brother Solomon?'

"'I don't know where he is,' I told them. I thought that they were going to kill me. I guess the Gestapo finally believed me because they stopped beating me and let me live.

"Moishe and I worked in the SS training camp as tailors for months," Michael continued. "Besides the one beating because of your letter, we were not treated very badly. In the summer of 1943, the SS notified us that they did not need so many tailors. The guards selected half of the tailors, including Moishe and me, and transferred us to an adjacent concentration camp called Szebnie. Life was very tough in Szebnie. Jews got beaten and shot everyday. Any misstep and the Nazis would take you to the forest and shoot you. If anyone resisted the Nazis, one hundred people would be killed for their defiance. Moishe and I somehow managed to survive alongside thousands of other Jewish people in Szebnie for the coming months.

"In November of 1943, the Soviet forces approached Szebnie. In the middle of the night, the Nazis forced all prisoners, including Moishe and me, to a railroad station where open cattle cars were waiting. We got separated at the train station. I never saw Moishe again. Nazis with guns forced me into a packed cattle car and locked the door from the outside.

"Almost no sunlight made it through the one small cattle car window. It was twenty degrees below zero outside. People in my car froze to death. After two and a half days in the freezing darkness, the train stopped. Nazi guards opened the doors. Gestapo ordered all prisoners off the train. Under heavy guard, I walked toward a Nazi camp surrounded in barbed wire. My eyes adjusted to the light. A sign hung above the entrance that read, 'Auschwitz.'

"SS stood assembling the new prisoners into two groups. Some prisoners were pointed to the left and the others were pointed to the right. Older people, crippled people, people with children, and young people were pointed to the left. Stronger looking, able-bodied working people were pointed to the right. The Gestapo pointed me to the left.

"I made a decision. I jumped over to the right side. The SS did not notice me because the selection was moving so fast. The thousands of people who had been pointed to the left were taken into gas chambers. They were gassed and then burned in crematoriums. I was taken to the reception barrack where I had to get completely undressed with the rest of the prisoners pointed to the right. Guards shaved our heads and tattooed a number on our left arm. They told us that we no longer had names. We would be known only as prisoner number such-and-such."

Michael stopped operating his sewing machine and pulled up his left sleeve. I could see the number, 160914, tattooed on his left arm. Michael rolled his sleeve back down and resumed operating his machine. He continued, "After receiving my number, I had to take a cold shower with the other prisoners. Guards then gave us thin striped pajama outfits. The Nazis did not care that it was twenty degrees below zero outside. They did not care that we were going to freeze to death or get pneumonia. They would kill us soon anyway. I was assigned to hard labor in Auschwitz for the next seven months.

"I was seventy-five pounds of skin and bones. I could not work anymore. I should have been taken to the gas chamber with the rest who could not work, but the prison supervisor liked me and noticed that I was not going to last. The supervisor transferred me to an adjacent camp called Auschwitz-Moniwitz where there was an IG Farben factory. I was assigned to work at the factory producing military supplies. I was able to slowly regain my health because I got more food at the factory.

"In January, 1945, the Soviet forces were getting close to Auschwitz. The Nazis did not want to leave any prisoners alive, so they rounded us all up. Alongside thousands and thousands of other prisoners including Jewish people, gypsies, and political prisoners from all nations, I marched west through snow, ice, and winter rain. SS shot anyone who did not follow their orders to march. If a prisoner fell down, they were shot and left lying in the road as the march continued on. We marched for the next two days and nights, stopping only when the guards wanted to rest. No food was distributed, but I had hidden a loaf of bread in my shirt that I nibbled on. Many had shoes with wooden soles, making it hard to walk in the snow. Fortunately, I had an un-matching pair of leather shoes, which had been taken from gassed inmates. It was still easier to walk in unmatched leather shoes than in wooden ones. It took all my strength and determination to keep up.

"Finally, after the two day death march, we arrived at another Nazi concentration camp. There was barely any available food and only standing room in the barracks. I found shelter in a shed where I huddled together with other prisoners for warmth. In the morning, many of the others in the shed were dead. I did not know how many had died before I arrived nor how many had died during the night.

"The next day, I was packed into another cattle car with other prisoners. Snow fell down as we traveled west into Germany. We stopped in a city on the outskirts of Berlin. After spending the night in a large hall, we were put on another train and transported into a concentration camp in Flossenburg. The Flossenburg camp was over-crowded with prisoners from other camps that had been evacuated to escape detection by the advancing Red Army. The food rations were meager. The only work was to sweep the com-pound or carry dead bodies.

"We stayed in the Flossenburg camp for five weeks. SS then marched us to a concentration camp in Leonberg. After another week, I was assigned to a nearby underground airplane factory to drill and rivet airplane wings. The Allies constantly dropped bombs on the underground factory, but it was well protected. Three weeks later, all prisoners from Leonberg were marched to another camp because the British and French armies approached from the west.

"After two more weeks, I was transported to a concentration camp in Bavaria with no barracks, only underground windowless rooms dug deep into the ground. The camp was divided by a wire fence. Women were on the other side. I could see that the womens' heads were also shaved. They looked malnourished. I had not seen a woman for a long time. Two weeks later, we were all transferred to another camp in Bavaria called Mildorf. I was assigned to work at the train station loading and unloading coal. Allied planes often bombed the trains. One day, the Allied planes flew especially low, firing machine guns. I dropped to the ground and saw bullets hitting the station all around me.

"In the end of April, 1945, SS forced me on a train that was loaded with war equipment and other prisoners. We had been traveling for several days before the Allies bombed the train. Many prisoners were killed and the train halted. I escaped and ran to a nearby village. I went into a German family's home and asked for food. They gave me some bread. I rested for an hour thinking that I might finally be free, but then an SS guard appeared. He rounded me up with the other surviving prisoners. We were forced to remove debris from the train tracks and then re-board the train.

"The train traveled toward Switzerland. In the middle of the night, we suddenly stopped. I could hear gunshots in the distance. After several hours, the train cars were unlocked. German officers with Red Cross emblems told us that the United States Army would be arriving soon. It was still nighttime, so we waited in the train. In the morning, the first American troops arrived.

"After my liberation, I remained in a displaced persons camp in Germany that was run by the United Nation Relief Organization. I made contact with our sister, Frances, here in Los Angeles. She sent me papers that I used to immigrate to the United States in 1946."

I listened to Michael as I continued to operate my sewing machine. Michael and I worked together at the women's coat factory in downtown Los Angeles for the next five years.

CHAPTER THIRTY-TWO

ལྩ

AMERICAN CITIZENSHIP

In 1955, after five years of working in the United States, I was eligible to become an American citizen. I told Michael that I wanted to change my name to Roosevelt Truman. "You must be crazy!" Michael said. "You should be proud to be a Berger." Michael was right. It was a stupid idea to change my name to Roosevelt Truman. When I registered for my citizenship papers, I decided to drop the "omon" from my first name. I would become Sol Berger.

I studied the United States Constitution as well as American laws and history. I passed the citizenship test. At the swearing in ceremony, a judge administered the United States Oath of Allegiance to a large group of new American citizens. I repeated after the judge and swore allegiance to the United States of America, swore not to be involved with the communist party, and swore to defend the United States against all enemies. I had no problem swearing allegiance to my new home. I had loved America before I even arrived. Compared to the anti-Semitism of pre-war Poland

and the times of Hitler, the American prejudices were nothing. America had finally given me freedom.

As a citizen, I decided that I did not want to work in the coat factory anymore. I wanted to start a different life. Michael and I pooled our money and purchased a tailor shop on Pico Boulevard and Swall Drive. We named our shop S & M Tailors. Michael and I were equal partners, but we did not make enough money to support our families. Michael continued to work at the factory downtown while I ran S & M Tailors.

Every day, I hated going to work. I had never liked being a tailor. I only became a tailor because my father had said to me so long ago, "If you're going to learn to be a tailor, it will save you from two things in your life: you'll never get rich and you'll never starve."

I ran S & M Tailors for five years until 1960, when I had had enough. I did not want to be a tailor anymore. My sister Eleanor had sold her liquor store and learned about my desire to find a new trade. Eleanor told Michael and me, "You two brothers should go ahead and buy a liquor store. It's a good way to make a living. I will teach you the business. You will start a different life. It costs $30,000 for a liquor store license. I know you don't have enough money, so I'll lend you the money that you need. I trust that you'll pay me back."

Michael and I followed our sister's advice. We sold all our tailoring machinery and pooled our savings. We had $15,000 between us. Eleanor lent us the rest. Michael and I purchased a liquor license and moved into a tiny store near the L.A. Coliseum on Hoover Street.

Our little junior market and liquor store made about $5,000 a month. Michael and I saved all profits and were able to quickly pay Eleanor back. We remodeled the inside of our store and purchased brand new equipment. Our business continued to grow. The tiny space became too small for us, so we rented the two adjacent buildings to use as a new department store. We sold not only liquor and food, but also clothing and all sorts of household items.

I enjoyed working with Michael. We were very close brothers. We stuck together and helped each other grow our business. We remained equal partners. Our only major issue was numerous robberies, so Michael and I each purchased guns for protection.

In the fall of 1963, I drove with Jackie, Marlene, and Gusta to the University of California at Berkeley to drop Jackie off at college. I was glad that I could afford to pay for Jackie's university education but was concerned about the many political demonstrations in Berkeley. I said to Jackie, "If you get into any trouble at college, come to me first, and I will help you. But if you get yourself arrested demonstrating against the United States of America, don't call me."

"Why not?" Jackie asked.

"Because in this country," I responded, "you have the opportunity to get an education and to live free. I did not have an opportunity to do that. Can you imagine yourself going through a lifetime with only a seventh grade education? Jewish people in Poland did not get to go to college. They had to go to work. That is why I will not bail you out if you get caught demonstrating against this wonderful country."

CHAPTER THIRTY-THREE

ℰ⅃

THE WATTS RIOTS

By 1965, Michael and I had eight employees and were grossing $100,000 each month. We used some of our profits to purchase another liquor store on Santa Barbara Avenue in Los Angeles, which is now called Martin Luther King Jr. Boulevard. Michael managed the new store while I ran the old one. Both stores did very well. Michael and I were on our way to becoming wealthy.

August 11, 1965. I was on vacation with Gusta, Jackie, and Marlene in Las Vegas. We were having a great time while Michael looked after both stores. I came back to our hotel room to find a message to contact Michael immediately. I called Michael and asked, "What's wrong?"

"Are you having a good time out in Las Vegas?" Michael responded.

"Wonderful!" I said. "It's so beautiful over here. We are in the pool all day."

"So…you don't know what's happening in Los Angeles? You have nothing to come back to."

"What do you mean I have nothing to come back to?"

"Don't you read newspapers or listen to the radio?"

"Who listens to the radio in Las Vegas? Who reads newspapers? You go to the casino to gamble or go to the pool."

"There are riots in Los Angeles."

"What do you mean, riots?"

"Well, people are rioting all over South Central Los Angeles. They're getting close to our Hoover store. You better come home." I hung up the phone and told the rest of my family to pack their belongings. We left right away. As we drove west toward Los Angeles, we listened to the news on the radio. Around midnight, they announced that the rioters were breaking into 4354 South Hoover Street. That was my store.

We drove all night and arrived safely at our home. In the morning, Michael and I decided to go down to Hoover Street to see whether we still had a store. We put a shotgun and a .38 revolver in the trunk of my car. There was a blockade of police and National Guard on La Brea and Rodeo. The police captain stopped us and asked, "Where are you going?"

"We are going to our store on Hoover Street," I said, "to see if there is anything left."

"You can't go to Hoover Street," the captain responded. "It's extremely dangerous."

"We still want to go," I said.

"Well, in that case, I want to ask you one question," the captain said. "Do you have firearms?"

"Yes," I told him.

"What arms do you have?"

"A shotgun and a .38 revolver."

"Where are they?"

"In the trunk."

"Are they loaded?"

"Yes, they're loaded."

"And you still want to go down to Hoover Street?"

"Yes. We insist. We need to see our store."

"Remember," the captain said, "I'm warning you not to go. But if you insist, I'll let you pass. However, I am telling you that you will most likely be attacked. Be prepared to use your firearms, or you will find yourself dead."

"We'll take our chances," I said. Michael and I took our guns out of the trunk. We drove carefully to our Hoover store. As we exited my car, I carried the .38 revolver on my belt like a policeman. Michael carried the shotgun on his shoulder.

Our store was demolished. All the merchandise had been stolen. There was nothing left. Some riotous thieves were still milling around our store looking for more things to steal. One of them said to me, "What are you doing here? Get out before I burn you completely."

I was so mad. "Just try it," I said, "and I'll blow your brains out." I took our liquor license and drove out of the riots safely with Michael. I never looked back. Fortunately, our other store on Santa Barbara Avenue was unharmed.

Michael and I ran our Santa Barbara Avenue store together for a little while, but we did not earn enough to support both of our families. I found another store in Burbank. Michael took the Burbank store and I kept the Santa Barbara Avenue store.

Even though there were quite a few robberies at my store, Gusta started to work as a cashier to help us save money. Fortunately,

Gusta and I were never harmed during a hold-up. My store was one of seven stores in the building on Santa Barbara Avenue. I continued to successfully grow my business and slowly purchased all six of the other stores. I eventually owned the entire building.

The Bar Mitzvah of Michael and Mildred's son, Ron. 1964. Michael (top left), Solomon (top right), sisters Rose and Eleanor (sitting, far left to right), Mildred (front center), and Gusta (far right)

CHAPTER THIRTY-FOUR

e⁄ɔ

BEVERLY HILLS REAL ESTATE AGENT

August 10, 1971. I could not go to work because I was at Cedars-Sinai hospital with kidney stones. Jackie had called the hospital every day from New York. Jackie, who had graduated from Berkeley and gotten married, was in New York doing medical research for NYU. We talked about his wife, Ethel, who was due to have their first baby any day. I had been in the hospital with terrible pains for six days. Doctors could only tell me to be patient. I kept drinking and drinking water and finally passed the kidney stones. The same day, Ethel gave birth to a baby girl named Tara. It was twenty-nine years to the day after the liquidation of Krosno when most of my family had been killed. I was now a grandfather.

I ran my store on Santa Barbara Avenue until 1975. I was able to support Marlene when she left home and attended college at UCLA and pay for Jackie's medical school in Bologna, Italy. In 1975, I was tired of the frequent hold-ups and increasing criminal activity around my store. I would change my life again. At the age of fifty-five, I sold my liquor store for $120,000 and enrolled at West L.A. Community College full time. I took courses in business law, accounting, and real estate.

In 1977, I received my real estate broker license. I would be a real estate man. When I told a friend who owned many properties about my new career, he said to me, "If you want to go into real estate, go to Beverly Hills. I will start you out with two listings. You must be in Beverly Hills."

"I don't fit into Beverly Hills," I responded. "I don't have enough knowledge or experience for someplace like that."

"You have more knowledge than all of them put together," my friend replied.

With newfound confidence, I applied for a job at Fred Sands Realtors in Beverly Hills. During the interview I said, "I have two pocket listings already. Between the two, they're worth more than two million dollars. I want to work in your office."

"You're in!" the interviewer said. That same day, I started to work at Fred Sands of Beverly Hills as a real estate agent. There were one hundred agents in the office, eighty percent women. By the end of my first year, I had sold over three million dollars worth of real estate and was the number one producer in the Beverly Hills office. I only worked as a listing agent and never worked with buyers. Working with buyers was a tough life, while listing agents controlled the transactions.

In 1981, the real estate market was suffering. Most of the divorced women in my office were unable to make a living for their families. I had several listings and continued to be successful, but many other agents in my office lost their jobs. Every morning, I dressed up in a nice suit. I walked into the office and said, "Good morning," to everyone in a bright, cheerful voice.

Jackie and Ethel's wedding. June 28, 1969. Jackie escorted by his parents

"What are you so frisky about?" the other agents sometimes responded.

"Well, its a beautiful day today," I said. "When I got up this morning, I did not need anybody to help me get out of bed. Breakfast was on the table. My mortgage is paid. What else do I have to worry about?"

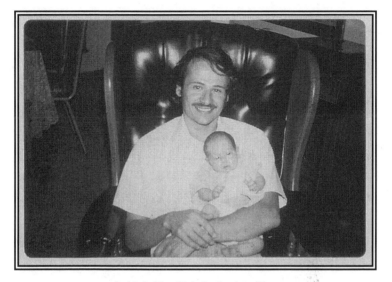

Jackie holding his baby daughter, Tara

One day, one of the divorced agents invited me to her house. She wanted to get close to me because she thought I was very rich. I refused her advances, but she did not want to give up.

"I have something better than you have in your house," she said.

"What you offer is worth nothing to me," I firmly told her. There was no way that I was going to break up my family. I loved Gusta and my children too much. Gusta was a gracious and loving wife. In my eyes, Gusta remained the most beautiful woman in the whole world.

I sold and bought many properties. Most were north of Santa Monica Boulevard in Beverly Hills. I flipped properties and made quite a bit of money. I used my earnings to buy Jackie and Marlene homes. I also financially supported Mr. and Mrs. Duchowski and their sons back in Krosno. The Duchowskis had saved my life more than once.

In the late 1980s, Michael sold his liquor store and began volunteering at the Los Angeles Museum of the Holocaust. He told his survival story to visitors of the museum. I never went near the Museum of the Holocaust because my pain was still too great. I did not talk to anyone about how I had survived. Even my own children did not know how Gusta or I had made it through the war. When Jackie and Marlene were just kids, they came home from school and asked, "Why don't we have any grandparents like all the other kids at school?"

We only told them, "They died in the war."

I did not want to share my stories with anybody. I did not want anybody else to have to suffer from my memories. The nightmares have not stopped since I arrived in America. In my nightmares, I fight the Nazis. Gusta sometimes wakes me up in the middle of the night because I am yelling. She says, "Stop it," as she shakes me awake. Other times, I kick off the covers and fall out of bed because I am running away from Nazis in my dream. I am grateful that when I wake up in the morning, I am able to function. I am grateful that I do not carry my dreams with me into the day.

Chapter Thirty-Five

A PROMISE

A t nighttime, as I lay in bed trying to fall asleep, I sometimes still
think about it. I cry for my grandfather. I was not with my
parents when the Germans took them, so I still think of them as alive.
But when I came back to the apartment in the ghetto where I found
only my grandfather's cap, that is the pain.

Not until many years after the war did I hear that Ukrainian
workers from our village killed my father the minute the Germans
arrived. I also heard that my mother escaped and worked on farms
pretending to be Catholic until 1944, when someone recognized her.
The Gestapo took her away. Even now, I still hope that somehow I
will see my parents alive someday.

I never again saw my brother or younger sister. When Germany
attacked, they both evacuated to Russia. Benjamin was later inducted into the Red Army. I heard he got wounded and came back
to Poland where he married a Catholic girl. They had some children,
but nobody knows what happened to them.

Dora survived the war in Russia as part of the youth communist *movement. In 1945, she came back to Tarnopol and spent some hours with my uncle Jacob. The aunt and uncle I had lived with as a teenager in Lodz had died during the war, but my uncle Jacob had survived. I will never forgive him, may he rest in peace, for not giving Dora my aunt's address in Israel. I do not know if Dora is dead or alive, but at least I found Mina. I talked to my sister every day.*

∾

In 1994, Michael was dying from cancer. We were still very close. Michael said to me, "Sol, for the last seven years I have been telling my story at the Holocaust Museum. I have also been a docent at the Museum of Tolerance since it opened last year. I tell the stories of the concentration camps and all the terrible things that happened during the war. I can't do it anymore. I'm sick. I know that I'm dying. I want you to take my place at the museum and tell the stories of what happened."

"I don't know what to say," I responded. "I've never been in a concentration camp. What would I say?"

"Say what you can and say what you know," Michael told me. "I want you to make me a promise. Before I die, promise me that you will continue with my presentations about the Holocaust. Promise me that you will tell the story of how we survived just like you promised our father. We both promised him that we would survive to tell the story of what the Nazis did to us."

Even though the pain was immense, I decided to continue with Michael's work at the museums. After fifty years, I realized that my story must be told. Deniers of the Holocaust were springing up all over the world. I could not sit by and watch history be repeated. I needed to fulfill my promise to my father.

"I promise," I said to Michael, "I will continue to tell our story."

A short time later, Michael died of lung cancer. At the age of seventy-five, I did not know how much longer I had left to live. I decided to retire and volunteer at the Museum of Tolerance. I walked from my house to the museum and told a representative, "I am a survivor, but I was never in a concentration camp. My brother, Michael, has told his story here since you opened. He can't tell his story anymore because he is dead. I made a promise that I would tell the story."

"Whatever you want to say will be perfect," the museum representative said. "We'll be very glad for you to be a volunteer."

I still did not know what I would say. I listened for three months to different presentations of Holocaust survivors at the museum. Most of them were Hungarians who told stories of how they lived in their nice homes until 1944 when the Gestapo came in and took them all to Auschwitz. The German SS murdered 500,000 Hungarian Jewish people. After hearing so many similar presentations, I decided that I had something to say. I could do as good a job there as anybody else.

Every week, I am still a volunteer speaker at the Museum of Tolerance and Los Angeles Museum of the Holocaust. It is not easy, but for almost twenty years, I have told my story. The museums send me to universities, high schools, churches, and synagogues. The more I speak, the better I get at sharing how I survived. But when I do my presentations, I only tell half of the story. The real story is not even the one I tell here. The real story is told in my dreams. Sometimes I think about how I dared to escape from the Gestapo through the barred window. I still cannot believe that I managed to survive.

I have been through depressive periods that lasted for years in America. I overcame these depressions by training myself with meditation. I used to be very explosive. If somebody wanted to hurt me, I wanted to fight back. After going through hell with Hitler and the Holocaust, I learned to meditate instead of responding with anger. When I am feeling stressed or depressed, I sit down, put on nice music, close my eyes, and rest my brain. I wake up from my meditation and everything bad is gone. I open fresh eyes.

If I am lucky, I open my eyes and see my Gusta sitting near me. From the moment I first saw her in Krakow, I have never stopped loving her. She is the most gracious, loving wife and the best mother, grandmother, and great grandmother. Gusta is my angel.

People ask me how I have stayed happily married to the same person for more than sixty years. I respond that when I am with Gusta, it feels like we got married yesterday. Nothing has changed for the worse. Everything has changed for the better.

Made in the USA
San Bernardino, CA
25 April 2017